AMERICAN INDIAN
PRAYER GUIDE

BY DANETTE MALOOF
WITH DEAN COZZENS
ILLUSTRATED BY LAURIE ARLOTTA

Published by
Sonlight Curriculum, Ltd.
8042 South Grant Way
Littleton, CO 80122-2705
(303) 730-6292 FAX (303) 795-8668
E-Mail: main@sonlight.com

For HELP: www.sonlight.com/forums/

ISBN 1-887840-50-8

Table of Contents

Map of Tribes

1 Maya	14 Iroquois	28 Pueblo
2 Taino/Arawak	15 Oneida	29 Apache
3 Powhatan	16 Huron/Ottawa	30 Navajo
4 Aztec	17 Potawatomi	31 Pomo
5 Wampanoag	18 Miami/Shawnee	32 Shoshone
6 Seminole	19 Cherokee	33 Nez Perce
7 Inuit	20 Chickasaw	34 Tlingit
8 Delaware	21 Osage	35 Chipewyan
9 Lumbee	22 Crow	36 Hawaiians
10 Natchez	23 Sioux	A Aleut
11 Choctaw	24 Blackfeet	B Salish
12 Ojibwa/	25 Cheyenne	C Chinook
Chippewa	26 Pawnee	D Chumash
13 Cree	27 Paiute/Ute	

AMERICAN INDIAN
PRAYER GUIDE

MAYA

Day 1

Did you know that way back when the prophet Isaiah was prophesying that Jesus would be born, there were already people living in America?

Some of these people lived in little villages in Central America. About 300 years after Jesus lived on the earth, these villagers, known as the Mayans (MY-uns), started coming together to form cities.

Each city had its own ruler. Cities that have their own rulers are like little states, so we sometimes refer to them as city-states.

◆◆◆

Prayer

Pray that the Mayans will know that Jesus,
the Prince of Peace, wants to be their Ruler.

Day 2

The Mayans built their cities out of stone. In their stone cities, the Mayans had many different jobs to do.

Farmers grew corn, beans, squash and chili peppers. Because they grew so much, they were able to feed many people. This meant that not everyone had to farm, hunt for animals, or gather food from wild plants, like the members of some other Indian tribes.

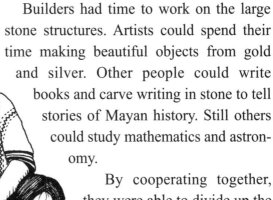

Builders had time to work on the large stone structures. Artists could spend their time making beautiful objects from gold and silver. Other people could write books and carve writing in stone to tell stories of Mayan history. Still others could study mathematics and astronomy.

By cooperating together, they were able to divide up the work and accomplish more than they would have if everyone had to gather food. Together the Mayans built a great civilization.

♦♦♦

Prayer

Praise the Creator for giving us minds with which to think and hands with which to work.

DAY 3

Civilizations do not last forever. They rise and fall. They appear great upon the earth, then fade away and are almost forgotten.

The time from 300 AD to 900 AD is called the classical period of the Mayans. That is when they were great upon the earth.

Then around 900 AD, the Mayan civilization came to a sad end. Builders stopped building, writers stopped writing, and stone-carvers stopped carving their history in the rocks.

We don't know what happened. Maybe there was a war, or perhaps the crops didn't grow well and people died of starvation. A terrible disease may have swept through the cities and killed many of the people. But whatever happened, some of the Mayans survived. Their descendants are still living today.

◆◆◆

Prayer

Pray that the Mayans will believe in Jesus and know that there will be no end to His Kingdom!

DAY 4

Christopher Columbus was sailing in the Gulf of Honduras in 1502 when he happened to meet some Mayan people in a canoe.

It was very hard for the Europeans to make their way through the thick jungle. Because it was so difficult, they did not often visit the Mayan people. Even though they did not visit very often, the Europeans exposed the Mayans to new diseases. When people are exposed many times to a certain illness, their bodies get used to fighting off that illness. But when a new disease suddenly comes to a society, people catch it!

That's what happened to the Mayans. They weren't used to the diseases carried by the Europeans. Many Mayans died of the strange European diseases, but others survived. Today, several million Mayans live in Guatemala and part of Mexico.

◆◆◆

Prayer

Pray that Christians will go to the Mayans and tell them that Jesus carried their sorrows when He died for them on the cross.

DAY 5

For hundreds of years, the Mayans had worshiped false gods. Spanish Christians destroyed many items that the Mayans used when they worshiped false gods.

Instead of telling the Mayans that Jesus wants to set them free from everything bad, and letting the Mayans decide what to do with their false gods, the Spaniards themselves decided what to do and what to destroy.

Then, because the hearts of the Mayans were not truly set free from worshipping false gods, some of them got even more mixed up. They mixed their old religious ways with the religious practices they learned from the Christians. This kind of religious mixture is called *syncretism*.

Today, many Mayans still do not know Jesus' love.

♦♦♦

Prayer
Pray that the Mayans will know the
love of Jesus, our Wonderful Counselor; that
they will be set free by the Mighty God; and
that they will worship the Eternal Father.

TAINO & ARAWAK

DAY **1**

It was Christmas Eve, 1492. Beneath the night sky, the island of the peaceful Taino (TIE-no) tribe lay still in the Caribbean Sea.

Then, to the surprise of Chief Guacanagari, a ship ran into the shore of the island! The chief and other Taino men rescued the Spanish sailors from the ship and welcomed them into their grass-covered huts. The ship was called the Santa Maria. The leader in charge was Christopher Columbus.

Columbus was confused about where he was. This island wasn't on his map. In fact, America wasn't on any world map yet. Columbus thought he was in the East Indies of Asia, so he named the island people "Indians."

The Tainos were confused about Columbus, too. They thought he came from heaven.

◆◆◆

Prayer

Pray that the Taino people will know that Jesus came from heaven, born as a baby, yet a King.

DAY **2**

Many Indian tribes are related to other tribes, like members of a large extended family. The friendly Tainos were part of a group of tribes called the Arawaks (AR-uh-wahks). The Arawak tribes lived on islands and on coastlands from North to

13

South America.

The name *Taino* means "good people." But the Tainos worshiped idols which represented evil spirits.

◆ ◆ ◆

Prayer

Pray that Jesus, the everlasting Light, will shine on the Taino and Arawak peoples, so they will turn away from darkness and evil, and turn to the Light!

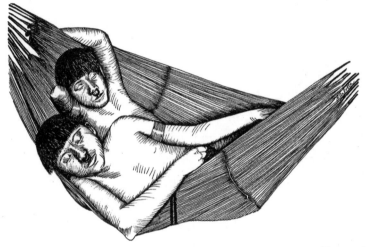

DAY 3

Some Tainos lived in Florida. They cooked their meat on a wooden rack over a fire. When they did this they called it a *barvacoa*. That's where we got our word *barbecue*.

Many English words are borrowed from other languages. In this case, the Spaniards borrowed *barvacoa* from the Taino. The English borrowed it from the Spaniards, and somewhere along the way it changed to *barbecue*.

The Spaniards learned other things from the Arawak people. For example, they learned how to make hammocks and how to grow tobacco, corn and potatoes. In turn, the Spaniards introduced horses and pigs to the Indians.

♦ ♦ ♦

Prayer

Praise our God who gives gifts to us—gifts
that we can share with others.

DAY 4

Chief Guacanagari and his people liked to trade with Indians who lived on other islands and on the mainland.

They had a system for their trading business. First, they would store up their extra goods in warehouses. Then they would carry these goods across the water in big canoes.

How excited Chief Guacanagari and his people were when they saw the huge Spanish ships. Surely there would be lots of things to trade!

But instead of trading fairly, the Spaniards stole from the Tainos, fought against them with weapons, and forced many of them into slavery.

♦ ♦ ♦

Prayer

Pray that the Taino and Arawak peoples will receive
the good gift of God's Son, and that their hopes
and fears will be answered in Him.

DAY 5

Today we say that Columbus discovered America. But what about the people who discovered Columbus?

When the Taino people first welcomed Columbus to their island, there were hundreds of thousands and maybe even millions of them living there. Because of the cruel treatment they received from their Spanish guests, within sixty years the tribe was gone from the island. Many Indians were killed by the Spaniards. Others were taken into slavery. Still others married Spaniards.

It wasn't long before the Tainos began to think that Christians were the cruelest people they had ever known. After all, they reasoned, weren't they Christians who were spilling the blood of people who had never done them wrong?

Tainos and Arawaks from other areas of the New World survived this awful period of history, and today a number of them live in Brazil, Cuba, Puerto Rico, New York, and New Jersey.

The island where the Tainos used to live is the same island where you will find Haiti and the Dominican Republic today.

◆ ◆ ◆

Prayer

Pray that the Tainos and Arawaks who are alive today will soon come to know that Emmanuel came not only to live with people on earth but to spill His blood for them on the cross.

POWHATAN

DAY 1

The home of the Powhatan Indians was a beautiful land of green trees in summer and multi-colored forests in autumn. There were plains where delicious crops could grow, and coast-lines bordering an ocean full of fish and shellfish.

Thirty groups of Indians banded together under Chief Wahunsonacock. Together they were called the Powhatan.

The Powhatans liked to build their towns near water like the Chesapeake Bay, or rivers that flowed into it. Not only did this give them access to fish, oysters and clams, but it also meant they had a good view of who was traveling along the river. They could see from a distance if any enemies were coming.

Besides fishing, the Powhatans also hunted animals and grew vegetables for food.

◆ ◆ ◆

Prayer
*Praise God, the Word, by whom all things on
the whole earth came into being.*

DAY 2

In 1607, a group of English settlers formed a colony in North America in a place they called Virginia. Virginia was a beautiful land, covered with large forests and coastal plains near the Atlantic Ocean. It was the land of the Powhatans.

But who really owned the land?

The Powhatans said, "Nobody owns it, but anybody (except our enemies) may use it."

The English said, "Whoever claims it owns it!"

English settlers claimed land—more and more land. They even killed Indians to get it, making themselves enemies of the Powhatans.

◆ ◆ ◆

Prayer

Pray that European Americans will not be selfish, wanting to get and take and own, but, rather, that they will receive what God has freely given: Jesus.

DAY 3

Pocahontas has long been remembered and her story retold many times.

Pocahontas was the daughter of Chief Wahunsonacock. She wanted to see peace between the Indians and the English, just like her father did. People who try to make peace are called diplomats.

Pocahontas was captured by the English in 1613 and taken to the city of Jamestown. While she was there, she accepted Jesus as her Savior and was baptized.

She married an Englishman named John Rolfe. Their marriage brought peace between the English and the Powhatans.

While traveling in England with her husband, Pocahontas got sick. She died there in 1617.

◆ ◆ ◆

Prayer

Pray that the Powhatans will know that Jesus, full of grace and truth, came from His Father willingly, in order to live among us.

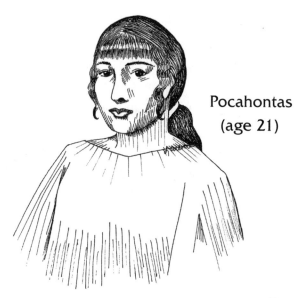

Pocahontas
(age 21)

DAY 4

After Pocahontas died, European settlers pushed the Indians further and further inland, in order to claim the land for themselves.

This was not only cruel and unfair to the Indians, but it made it harder for them to survive. Being further away from the waterways meant they had to depend more on farming and less on fishing. This, in turn, meant they had to move more often in order to plant new fields. It also meant they did not have as clear a view of enemies who were coming to attack.

Peace gave way to terrible fighting between the settlers and the Powhatans. By 1675, most of the Powhatans had disappeared. Today, some Powhatans still live in Virginia, Pennsylvania and New Jersey.

◆ ◆ ◆

Prayer
Pray that the remaining Powhatans will know that when the Lamb of God died, He made it possible for us to live in peace with God.

DAY 5

Chief Wahunsonacock once said to English Captain John Smith, "Why will you take by force what you may quietly have by love?... We are... willing to give you what you ask, if you come in a friendly manner, and not... to make war upon an enemy."

The "clash of culture," the differences between the culture of the Powhatans and the culture of the English, had brought about a very real physical clash that cost many people their lives.

◆ ◆ ◆

Prayer

Pray that European Americans and Powhatans will humbly receive the grace and love of God through Jesus Christ.

AZTEC

DAY 1

If you were watching a video about the Aztec Indians, you would see a very large empire in what is now called Mexico. The Aztec empire stretched from the Gulf of Mexico to the Pacific Ocean.

As the video scanned the area, you would see the Aztecs attacking cities and bringing them under Aztec control.

In more peaceful places, you would see Aztec families eating tortillas and tamales. Out in the fields you would see crops of corn, beans, tomatoes and chili peppers. Every so often a dog or a turkey would run across the screen.

◆◆◆

Prayer

Pray that God, who sees even the hearts of people, will speak to the hearts of Aztec descendants.

DAY 2

If you rewound the "video" we talked about yesterday back to the beginning, you could watch the Aztecs in the early stages of their civilization.

In about 1168, they came into what we now know as Mexico. For many years, they wandered about as hunters and warriors. Finally, in 1325, they found what they believed was the perfect place to build a village. It was in the place we know as Mexico City

The Aztecs believed they had heard a prophecy about this spot long before. They had certain prophecies that were part of their culture, and one was about the place where they should build a village. The prophecy was not in the Bible; they didn't know the true God. But they believed the prophecy, so they didn't mind that their special spot was a swamp.

By working hard, the Aztecs built islands in the swamp. Then they built buildings on the islands. Their village became a city, with thousands of stone buildings, lots of canals, and 300,000 people—bigger than the largest cities in Europe at that time. It was called Tenochtitlan, the capitol of the Aztec empire.

◆ ◆ ◆

Prayer

Pray that Aztec descendants will read the Bible
and see how God fulfilled many true prophecies.

DAY 3

There are some parts of the Aztec "video" that you would not want to see, like the part right after they captured prisoners during their battles.

Besides taking prisoners as *slaves*, the Aztecs killed many of them in the stone temples of Tenochtitlan. They thought that their gods wanted them to kill their prisoners.

The Aztecs did a lot of evil things for their false gods. They thought they were doing right.

◆ ◆ ◆

Prayer

Pray that the true and holy God will set Aztec descendants
free from doing wrong and thinking it's right.

Motecuhzoma
(Montezuma)

DAY 4

The sequel to the Aztec "video" stars a Spaniard named Cortez. In 1519, Cortez and 400 Spanish soldiers invaded the Aztec empire. They made friends with people who didn't like the Aztecs. With the help of their new friends, the Spaniards defeated the Aztecs.

The Aztecs had two big problems. First, they had never seen horses or guns before, while the Spaniards had both. The bows and arrows the Aztecs used were no match against the Spaniards' weapons.

Second, the Aztecs thought Cortez, with his light skin, might be their god Quetzalcoatl. When they finally figured out that Cortez wasn't their god, it was too late. By 1521, the

Spanish had completely taken over the Aztec Empire. They destroyed Aztec temples and books and made the Aztecs their slaves.

The Spanish called the area New Spain. Today we call it Mexico.

◆ ◆ ◆

Prayer

Pray that Aztec descendants in Mexico will know Jesus, who is God and yet a man.

DAY 5

After the Spanish took over, some Aztecs married Spanish people. Now many Mexicans are part Spanish and part Indian.

Mexico City stands where Tenochtitlan used to be. The Aztec language, Nahuatl, is still spoken among some of the farmers living in villages around Mexico City.

There really is a video in that uses the Nahuatl language. But the video is not about the Aztec civilization. It's about Jesus!

Since different groups of people speak the Nahuatl language in different ways, called dialects, the *Jesus* Film has been translated into four different dialects of Nahuatl.

◆ ◆ ◆

Prayer

Pray that many people who speak Nahuatl will see the Jesus *Film and believe in Jesus as their Savior.*

WAMPANOAG

DAY 1

In 1615, a strange journey began for an Indian named Squanto.

He was captured by an English trader named Mr. Hunt. Then he was taken to Spain where Mr. Hunt sold him as a slave to another Englishman. The Englishman who bought him took him to England and set him free. Finally, in 1619, Squanto found a ship to take him back to America.

Squanto was a member of the Pawtuxet band of Wampanoag (womp-uh-NO-ag) Indians. When he got to America, he wanted to go home to his people, but he discovered that his entire village of Pawtuxets had died from disease.

Because of his strange journey, Squanto's life had been spared!

◆◆◆

Prayer
Thank God for taking what an English slave trader did and working it out for good in Squanto's life.

DAY 2

In 1620, a group of Pilgrims landed at a place they called New Plymouth.

Wampanoag Indians lived in their dome-shaped wigwams not far from New Plymouth. One day, the Pilgrims were surprised when an Indian walked into their village and spoke to them in English!

The Indian's name was Samoset (SAM-uh-set). He was a friend of Squanto. Squanto had helped him learn English.

Samoset introduced the Pilgrims to Squanto, and Squanto came to live with the white people in the very place where his own tribe had once lived!

♦♦♦
Prayer
Thank God for how He brings people
together according to His purpose.

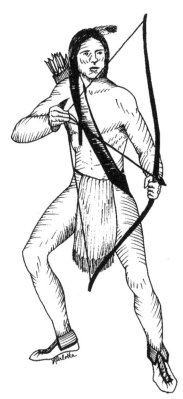

DAY 3

In the 1600s, a chief ruled the "people to the east," the Wampanoag people. The chief's name was Massasoit (mas-uh-SOYT).

Massasoit and his people lived along the coast of the Atlantic Ocean, where parts of Massachusetts and Rhode Island are today. Massasoit was introduced to the Pilgrims by Samoset.

In 1621, Massasoit and the Pilgrims made a peace agreement or treaty. They agreed to live as brothers and to protect each other.

Massasoit is remembered today as "Protector and Preserver of the Pilgrims."

♦♦♦
Prayer
Thank God for using Chief Massasoit to protect the Pilgrims.

DAY 4

In the Autumn of 1621, the Pilgrims and Indians shared what we think of as the first American Thanksgiving feast.

The Pilgrims were thankful that God had spared their lives. God had spared Squanto's life by letting him be taken away from his people so he wouldn't catch the disease that had killed them. Then God used Squanto to help save the Pilgrims' lives. Squanto taught the Pilgrims how to fish and how to raise crops like corn for food.

Even though the Indians and Pilgrims had both been through many difficulties, they gave thanks to God for His provision and protection.

♦♦♦
Prayer
Thank God for using Squanto to help the
Pilgrims and to spare many lives.

DAY 5

In 1662, things changed. Chief Massasoit died.

During Massasoit's lifetime, the Wampanoags and Pilgrims had lived at peace with one another, according to their peace treaty.

After Massasoit died, Massasoit's oldest son Philip became the Wampanoag leader. Philip and his people became more and more angry because the whites had broken many of their other treaties with the Indians. Broken treaties are broken promises:

very serious indeed.

Finally, in 1675, peaceful times ended, as the Wampanoags went to war against the white settlers. Philip and many Wampanoags were killed. Some who survived were captured and sold as slaves. Today, about 700 Wampanoags live in Massachusetts.

◆◆◆

Prayer

Thank God for never breaking His promises. Ask Him to forgive us for not always keeping ours. Pray that the Wampanoags, as well as we ourselves, will know God's faithfulness, even His faithfulness to forgive.

SEMINOLE

DAY 1

"Wild!" "Runaway!" These words have been used to describe the Seminole (SEM-ih-nole) people. The word *Seminole* comes from the Spanish word *cimarron* (SIM-uh-ron), which means "wild" or "runaway."

The Seminole Indians have always loved freedom. Sometimes they would run away to be free. Sometimes they would fight.

God made everyone with a free will. But some peoples, like the Seminoles, seem to have stronger wills than others.

In the 1500s, the Seminoles fought the Spaniards with arrows that were hard enough to pierce Spanish armor! In the 1700s and 1800s, Seminoles living in Georgia fled from white settlers and moved into what is now Florida.

◆◆◆
Prayer
Praise God for giving us free will, so that we can choose to follow Him.

DAY 2

The Seminoles weren't the only ones who ran away to be free. In the early 1800s, black slaves fled to Florida to escape slavery. The Seminoles helped the escaped slaves by giving them work to do and food to eat.

Florida was not part of the United States at that time. It was controlled by Spain.

In 1817, American General Andrew Jackson was sent to fight the Seminoles in order to stop black slaves from running away. He was also sent to take Florida away from Spain.

Jackson and his troops went into Seminole villages, took what they wanted, and set fire to the villages. Spain lost control over Florida, and Florida became part of the United States.

◆◆◆

Prayer

Pray that the Seminoles will know that God wants to give them even greater freedom and protection than they were able to give to runaway black slaves.

DAY 3

Andrew Jackson became President of the United States in 1828. While he was President, the Indian Removal Act was passed. This Act ordered five Indian tribes, including the Seminoles, to leave their homes and land.

Some of the Seminoles refused to leave Florida; instead they fought the American army. In this war, one U.S. soldier died for every two Seminoles who were forced to move west. About 3,000 Seminoles started on the journey to "Indian Territory," what we know as Oklahoma.

The Indians were not given enough food or blankets. Many died of starvation, disease, and exposure to the weather. No wonder this forced move was called the "Trail of Tears"!

◆◆◆

Prayer

Pray that the Seminoles will know that Jesus went through unspeakable agony when He gave His life for us, and that because of His shed blood there can be forgiveness for all sin.

Osceola
Seminole warrior
and war chief

DAY 4

Today there are over 15,000 Seminoles living in America, mostly in Florida and Oklahoma.

Even when they stay in one place, the Seminoles seem to be "on the move." They are a very hard-working people.

Many years ago Seminoles were busy farmers who raised corn, squash, tobacco, sweet potatoes and melons. They also gathered fruit, hunted and fished. They even hunted alligators! Later they raised cattle. Seminole children were trained to work from an early age.

Today, many Seminoles are farmers and ranchers. Others construct buildings, and some even build airplanes. In Florida, some Seminoles entertain tourists by wrestling alligators.

♦ ♦ ♦
Prayer
Thank God for the hard-working Seminoles.
Pray that they will find their rest in Jesus.

31

DAY 5

Like many other Indian tribes, the Seminoles were forced by the United States government to live on pieces of land called reservations. Reservations are reserved only for the use of Indians.

Today, there are many churches on Seminole reservations. However, many Seminoles still go to see traditional medicine men. Their "medicine" often combines the use of herbs and roots—which God has made for our benefit—with prayers to evil spirits.

Those who look for help from medicine men need to understand that they cannot combine good and evil and call it good. They need to be set free from the evil spirits!

◆ ◆ ◆
Prayer
*Pray that the Seminoles will truly
be set free by Jesus Christ.*

INUIT

DAY 1

Did you ever wake up when it was still dark and wonder when the sun would come up? In the winter, Inuits (IN-yoo-its) get up when it is still dark. They go to bed when it's dark. They do a lot of things in the dark, because it's almost always dark. But in the summer, it's almost always light where the Inuits live.

This is because the Inuits live close to the top of the world. Some Inuits live in Alaska; some in Siberia, Russia; others in Greenland; and many live in northern parts of Canada, like the new territory of Nunavut.

Because the Earth is tilted on its axis, the land of the Inuits is tilted away from the sun during the winter. In the summer, it is tilted toward the sun. Yet although the winters are very cold, the summers never get hot.

The Inuits are sometimes referred to as Eskimos.

♦♦♦
Prayer
Praise God who prepared the sun, who formed light and created darkness, and who made summer and winter.

DAY 2

In spite of the cold climate, the Inuits are generally very warmhearted—friendly, hospitable and happy.

For hundreds of years, they have been a communal people,

doing things together as a community. They have lived near each other, traveled together, and told stories to each other.

The men go on hunting expeditions together. On land, they hunt caribous, polar bears, foxes, wolves and mountain sheep. On water, they travel in boats to catch fish and hunt animals like whales, seals, walruses and dolphins.

The Inuits' survival often depends upon their sticking together. How would you like to be swishing over the snow in a dog sled, all by yourself, with a pack of wolves hunting you?

♦♦♦
Prayer
Pray that many Inuits will come to know that they can have the best fellowship with each other when they walk in the light of Jesus.

DAY 3

Hunting and fishing are very important to the Inuit people. They depend on meat for food, and they also use animal furs and skins. Animal skins are used to make canoe-shaped boats called kayaks, and furs make warm coats.

The sale of furs and skins has been an international business for the Inuits. In about 984, the Inuits of Greenland met some Vikings from northern Europe. They began a trading relationship. Inuits in the west started trading with the Russians in 1741.

Trading relationships benefit both sides because they can each share in what the other has.

♦♦♦
Prayer
Pray that the Inuits will enjoy a close relationship with God and receive His richest blessings.

DAY 4

When God created people, He created them with a need to know Him. But when people don't know Jesus as the Light of the world, they often worship something else.

Not knowing the God who made the animals, the Inuits thought they should pray to animals.

In the 1800s, some Christians from Germany, called Moravians (mo-RAY-vee-uhns), came to the Inuits. The Moravians were "on fire" for God; they sent missionaries all over the world. They also started a 24-hour prayer chain, with different people praying at all times around the clock. This continued for almost 100 years!

The Moravians wanted to be lamps for Jesus and "reach those in spiritual darkness."

♦ ♦ ♦
Prayer
Praise God for the Moravians who brought the light of Christ to the dark land of the Inuits!

DAY 5

God answers prayer!

Recently in Canada, one village of 500 Inuit people decided to turn to God.

The villagers had been facing serious problems such as alcoholism, drugs, physical abuse, and suicides among teenagers. Finally they cried out to God.

They gathered up their alcohol, drugs, heavy metal music, and other things that had kept them from God, and put it all in a big pile. They poured gasoline on the heap. Then, together, as a community, they set it on fire! All the people cheered as flames shot into the air. It was a huge bonfire. It produced light and heat like they had never known!

The "fire" of God's power has been spreading to other Inuit villages. Police have noticed fewer crimes being committed, and Police Chiefs in 125 Canadian cities have watched a video which tells about God's work among the Inuit people.

◆◆◆
Prayer
Praise God for calling Inuits out of
darkness into His marvelous light!

DELAWARE

DAY 1

The Delaware Indians call themselves the Lenape (luh-NAH-pay). They are the grandfathers.

A whole tribe of old men? No. But many other Indian tribes on the East Coast thought of the Lenapes as grandfathers.

The tribes that felt this way all spoke the same Algonquian (al-GONG-kee-en) language, and they all thought of themselves as a large extended family. The Lenapes were thought to be the original people in the family. And the other tribes respected the Lenapes as if they were their grandfathers.

Because of this, the Lenapes were often asked to help settle disagreements between the other tribes.

◆ ◆ ◆
Prayer
*Pray that many Lenapes will know the Father who
is in heaven and respect His Name above all.*

DAY 2

Besides women, children and young men, there always were some old men among the Lenape people. Some of these old men were leaders of villages or other, smaller groups within the Lenape tribe. These leaders were called "The Old and Wise Men of the Nation." Altogether, there were about 200 of these "Old and Wise Men."

The Lenapes also had a chief, but the chief didn't make all the decisions. Many of the important decisions were made by the "Old and Wise Men" when they met together as a council.

This type of representative leadership is similar to the kind of representative government the United States has adopted.

◆ ◆ ◆
Prayer
Pray that the Lenapes will desire God's leadership, His kingdom and His will.

DAY 3

The Lenape people lived where Delaware, New Jersey, New York, and eastern Pennsylvania are today. Families lived in round, bark-covered houses.

The tribe originally lived near a river which they called Lenape-Wihituck. Europeans called it the Delaware River, and they gave the name Delaware to the Lenape Indians.

In 1682, across the ocean, King Charles II of England decided to give the land of

Pennsylvania to a Christian man named William Penn. However, Penn did not believe the king of England could take the Indians' land away from them and give it to someone else. So he purchased southeast Pennsylvania from the Delaware for a fair price.

♦♦♦
Prayer
*Pray that the Delaware Indians will know
that God has the authority to give us
everything we need, each day and forever.*

DAY 4

The city of Philadelphia was built on the land that William Penn bought from the Delaware Indians. Philadelphia is where the United States Constitution was signed.

The men who signed the Constitution of the United States are called the "founding fathers" of the United States.

Just like "the Old and Wise Men of the (Lenape) Nation" would meet together to make important decisions for their whole nation, our founding fathers met to make important decisions for the United States.

William Penn had purchased from the "grandfather tribe" the land on which America's founding fathers signed a very important document. The United States Constitution would be used to settle disagreements for centuries to come.

♦♦♦
Prayer
*Pray that the Delaware Indians, and we ourselves, will be
led by our Heavenly Father who is able to settle
any problem and help us make right decisions.*

DAY 5

William Penn was a Quaker Christian. He, like other Quakers, wanted to set a good example for the Indians by treating them fairly.

Another Christian who influenced the Delawares was David Brainerd, called "the Apostle to the Indians." Brainerd poured out his heart to God in prayer for the Indians, and he saw many of them put their faith in Christ. In 1747, Brainerd died at the age of 29.

In about 1740, Moravian Christians also came to the Delawares. When the Delawares moved further west because there were so many white settlers in the east, the Moravian Christians went with them.

Today, Delaware Indians live in Oklahoma, New York, Wisconsin, New Jersey, Kansas, and in Ontario, Canada.

◆ ◆ ◆
Prayer
"Praise You, Father, for those among the Delaware Indians who have come to You through Jesus. Yours is the kingdom, and the power, and the glory, forever. Amen."

LUMBEE

DAY ONE

The Lumbee (LUM-bee) Indians live in southeastern North Carolina. As far back as anyone can remember, they have been living in the same place for centuries.

When the King of England was giving out land in America, the Lumbee asked him to give their land to *them* so they could keep living on it. The King at that time was George II, and he agreed to let the Lumbee have their land.

White settlers did not try to take the Lumbees' land away from them, because King George II had given it to the Indians. Besides, the land was in a swampy area, and white settlers did not want that.

The United States has never tried to remove the Lumbees from the place where they have been living.

◆◆◆
Prayer
Thank God, the Lord of all the earth, for
providing a special place for the Lumbees to live.

DAY TWO

The reason the Lumbees talked to King George about their land was because they recognized the king's authority. He was the one in charge at that time. The tribe knew they would be much better off if they developed some kind of relationship with the king.

The Lumbees recognized the same thing about God. Sometime in the 1700s or 1800s, many of them decided to submit themselves to God as their authority.

Christianity became the "traditional" religion of the Lumbees. That means that the Lumbees, as a tribe, consider Christianity to be their own religion.

◆◆◆
Prayer

Thank God that many Lumbees recognize His authority, that they acknowledge the Lord Himself as their God.

DAY THREE

Believe it or not, the land on which the Lumbees live no longer belongs to the Lumbee tribe.

Yes, they have lived there for hundreds of years. Yes, the king of England said they could have the land. But the United States is now independent from Great Britain and no longer under the authority of the king or queen of England.

In the United States, the government has given many tribes reservation land. But in order for tribes to be given reservation land, they need to be recognized by the United States government. The Lumbees are not legally recognized by the U.S. government.

If a tribe is to be legally recognized, the government of the United States has to be willing to talk to the leaders of the Indian tribe as government leaders; it has to be willing to treat the tribe as an independent nation within the larger nation of the United States. Although the United States recognizes the Lumbee people as Indians, it does not recognize the Lumbees as a nation.

The Lumbee tribe is as large as other tribes. There are over 50,000 Lumbees who are alive today. Many still live in Robeson County, North Carolina.

◆◆◆
Prayer

Pray that the Lumbees will remember that their identity does not come from a government. It is God who has made them—not they themselves, and not anyone else.

DAY FOUR

The Lumbees recognize the value of hard work and also the value of people. Relationships are important to the Lumbees, and they love their families.

Lumbee families are very close. There is a closeness not only between the people in each individual family, but between many families as they relate to each other.

The relationships between Lumbee families help to make their society strong.

◆◆◆
Prayer

Pray that Lumbee Christians will rejoice that they are members of God's family; that they are His people.

DAY FIVE

The Lumbees have worked hard to find out about their

ancestors. It has not been an easy task. Much of the history of the Lumbee people has been lost.

Yet that doesn't keep them from building a strong community today. The churches, businesses and schools of the Lumbee people help their whole community, and the county in which they live.

Though the Lumbees may not be able to tell a lot of stories about their fathers' fathers, they can still leave a rich heritage for their children's children.

◆ ◆ ◆
Prayer
Praise the Lord, whose loving-kindness is everlasting,
and whose faithfulness is to all generations.

NATCHEZ

DAY ONE

What was the largest city in the United States before 1800? Here are some hints: It covered more than 11 square miles. It was near what is now St. Louis. It had a downtown and five suburbs. Can you guess?

It was the city of Cahokia (kuh-HO-kee-uh). The 30,000 people who lived in Cahokia were Natchez Indians. The Natchez were called "mound builders" because they piled up huge mounds of dirt.

In Cahokia, they built a mound that was over ten stories high. It took them from about 900 to 1100 AD to build such a big hill. They built a temple way up at the top.

◆◆◆
Prayer
Pray that the Natchez will know God,
who knows everything about them.

DAY TWO

There were other mound builders besides the Natchez, but we don't know very much about these other tribes. Where did the people go? Who are they today? Why did they build such big mounds? These questions are hard to answer.

We do know, however, that the mound builders lived a long time ago (probably from 1800 BC to 1500 AD), and that they lived in cities and villages.

Some of the mounds look like the walls of a fort. Others had temples on them or thrones where powerful kings would sit. Some mounds were graves of important leaders. Things that belonged to the leaders were often buried with them. Today we call these very old belongings *artifacts*. The artifacts give us clues about the culture of the mound builders.

Most of these mounds are found in the Midwest and along the Mississippi River.

◆◆◆
Prayer
Pray that the descendants of the mound builders
will know God, from whom they can never hide.

DAY THREE

We know more about the Natchez than the other mound builders. It seems that the city of Cahokia was inhabited even after the villages of other mound builders were deserted.

The Natchez traded their goods with other Indians in North America, and even Central America!

In their religious practices, the Natchez were similar to the Aztecs of Central America. And the temples the Natchez built were similar to the temples of the Mayans and Aztecs. Maybe they learned from each other.

The king of the Natchez was called the Great Sun. He sat on a throne on top of a high mound and wore a crown of swan feathers with red tassels. On a different mound one could find priests in a temple. They had no crowns and no hair. Their heads were shaved. The priests did not know the true God, and neither did the people.

♦♦♦
Prayer
Pray that the Natchez will know the
true God who is high above all.

DAY FOUR

It was the custom of early Christian missionaries to ask the Indians to come away from their villages, to a separate place, in order to learn about God.

Often the missionaries would build a chapel and other buildings on a separate piece of land. They called these places missions. They encouraged Indians to come to the missions to attend church services and sometimes even to live.

The French built a mission near the Natchez people in 1706. Soon afterward, they built a trading post and a fort called Fort Rosalie.

The Natchez and the French trusted each other, traded with each other, and lived at peace with one another.

♦♦♦
Prayer
Pray that the Natchez will know God,
who wants to meet them where they are.

DAY FIVE

The peace between the Natchez and the French lasted only 23 years. A French governor, who was very selfish, decided he would like to have a plantation in the place where Cahokia stood. He ordered the Natchez to leave their Great Village.

The Natchez were angry with the greedy governor. They attacked Fort Rosalie in 1729. They killed the governor as well as a missionary and some soldiers.

The French later attacked and defeated the Natchez. Some of the Natchez were sold into slavery. Others went to live with other tribes. Today most Natchez descendants live in Oklahoma among other Indian tribes.

◆◆◆
Prayer
Pray that the Natchez and other Indians will know God, who is always fair and just, holy, and full of love and compassion.

CHOCTAW

DAY ONE

The Choctaw lived in the Southeastern United States, mainly in Mississippi, as well as Alabama, Georgia and Louisiana. They were peaceful people. According to their legends, they were descendants of mound builders.

Whites called the Choctaw and four other tribes—the Cherokee, Chickasaw, Creek and Seminole—the "Five Civilized Nations."

The governments of these tribes were similar to the government of the United States. They all had constitutions and three parts to their governments similar to our president, congress, and courts (what we call the "executive, legislative, and judicial branches"). The five tribes also had their own schools and colleges.

White Americans thought of themselves as civilized. Since the five tribes ran their affairs in a manner similar to the way the whites did, the whites said that these tribes were civilized, too.

♦♦♦
Prayer
Pray that God will help us not to think
of ourselves as better than others.

DAY TWO

The Choctaw fought on the side of the Americans in the Revolutionary War. They also helped out in the War of 1812, serving under General Andrew Jackson.

Yet, after Jackson became president, he didn't help the Choctaws. Instead, he signed the Indian Removal Act which ordered the Five Civilized Nations to leave their homes and move west.

The Choctaw were the first to move to Indian Territory. A Choctaw man named the new territory *Oklahoma*, which means "red people."

One out of every four Choctaws died on the way to Oklahoma. After the remaining Choctaws had settled, whites moved west and took even more land away from them.

♦♦♦
Prayer
Pray that the Choctaws will realize what
Jesus' death on the cross means for them.

DAY THREE

The U.S. government forced the Choctaws to divide into groups for the move west. Then it forced all the groups to move in the middle of the winter. Some Choctaws rode on boats or wagons part of the way. Others were forced to wade through miles of ice cold flood and swamp water.

Most of the Choctaws had to walk the last 150 miles—either that or be carried. Babies and very young children were carried. But older children and adults who couldn't be carried either walked or died. Bodies were piled up and burned; the ground was too frozen to bury them.

By the end of the "Trail of Tears," thousands of Choctaws had died from disease, cold weather, and lack of food and clothing. Those who survived arrived in their new wilderness home with practically nothing left.

◆◆◆
Prayer

Pray for God's strength, wisdom and compassion on the part of white Americans to confront this wicked part of our history. Pray too that Native Americans will be able to forgive.

DAY FOUR

A few years before the Indian Removal Act was signed, Christian missionaries went to the Choctaws. The Indians seemed ready to believe in Jesus. They already knew about the Great Flood, even before the missionaries came.

Because of the missionaries, Choctaws could hear the gospel and believe in Jesus as their Savior.

Happily, many Indians who started on the "Trail of Tears" probably walked right into heaven! Sadly, they should have never been forced to endure such a "Trail of Tears" here on earth.

Today, Choctaw pastors and evangelists tell others about hope in Jesus.

◆◆◆
Prayer
*Pray that white Americans will be
sensitive to the pain of Native Americans.*

DAY FIVE

Civilized people are supposed to treat their neighbors with kindness and justice.

Someone once asked Jesus, "Who is my neighbor?" (Luke 10:29, NASB). To answer the question, Jesus told a story about a man who set out on a journey. Robbers came upon the man, stripped him of his clothes, "beat him, and went off leaving him half dead" (vv. 30*ff*). A priest and a Levite both walked by without stopping to help.

Indians were robbed of their land and forced to go on a long journey. On the way, they got so cold and hungry and sick that thousands of them died.

This, together with other injustices suffered by the Indians, has caused many of them to feel hopeless. It is the kind of feeling you would feel if you were robbed, stripped, beaten, and left half dead.

◆◆◆
Prayer
*"Father, help us to love our neighbors, the
Indians, and to show that love by our actions."*

OJIBWA/CHIPPEWA

DAY ONE

If you were paddling a canoe on a lake in Minnesota, you might see wild rice growing in the water. But be careful, there are rules about picking it!

If you are within the boundaries of a Chippewa (CHIP-eh-wuh) Indian reservation, you must be a member of the tribe or live on the reservation in order to harvest the rice.

If the lake used to belong to the Chippewas but is not part of the Chippewa Reservation, according to a treaty signed in 1837, you might be permitted to gather some wild rice. But there are still rules about when and how to harvest it. The rules are made by officials of both the State of Minnesota and the Chippewa Indian tribe.

If you are in some other part of Minnesota and are not a Chippewa, you must be a Minnesota resident, with a wild rice harvester's license, and it must be the right time of year and the right time of day.

Otherwise, just buy some wild rice in a store.

◆◆◆
Prayer
*Thank God for creating a beautiful land
and nutritious food for the Chippewa people.*

DAY TWO

You may have noticed that this article is titled "Ojibwa/Chippewa." That is because *Chippewa* is a name that the Europeans gave to the tribe that called itself the Ojibwa (o-JIB-way). The Ojibwa lived in parts of what are now Michigan, Wisconsin, Minnesota, North Dakota, and Ontario, Canada.

In Minnesota, some of the land that the Ojibwa lived on is called the Boundary Waters Canoe Area. You need a canoe to get around in the Boundary Waters. The land is found only here and there between the all the lakes!

The Ojibwa/Chippewa have long been known as skilled canoe builders. They are also very good fishermen.

Many lakes in the Boundary Waters Canoe Area have names which came from the Ojibwa/Chippewa language.

◆ ◆ ◆
Prayer
Thank God for the many
skills and abilities He has given the Ojibwa/Chippewa.

DAY THREE

In 1825, a treaty was signed. The purpose of the treaty was supposedly to ensure peace between the Ojibwa/Chippewas and the Sioux.

The treaty drew a line through the middle of Minnesota, Wisconsin and Michigan, dividing them north to south. The land to the north was given to the Chippewas, and the southern portion to the Sioux.

The real reason for the treaty, however, was to help the Indians get used to the idea of boundary lines. U.S. officials wanted the tribes to start thinking of land as something that has defined limits and belongs to someone.

The Indians did begin to think this way. Then, the United States moves the lines so that the Indians ended up with less and less land.

♦♦♦
Prayer
Pray that white Americans, especially Christians, will realize how unfairly Indians have often been treated so that we, too, can pray that justice will be done in their behalf.

DAY FOUR

Today, there are over 104,000 Ojibwa/Chippewas in the United States. Many also live in Canada.

Some live within the boundaries of reservations. Others live in cities along with people of different nationalities.

Those on the reservations live more like their ancestors lived—hunting, fishing, gathering wild rice and berries, making arts and crafts, or harvesting wood and processing it in lumber mills.

◆ ◆ ◆

Prayer*Pray that Christians living near the
Ojibwa/Chippewas
will share the love of Jesus with them.*

DAY FIVE

Some Ojibwa/Chippewas believe in Jesus as their Savior. They help others to grow in Christ. Craig Smith is a Chippewa who gives leadership to Native American churches and pastors across the United States. He and other Native Christian leaders want to help Indian Christians live according to the Bible.

Indians who believe in Jesus need to decide what to do about traditional Indian beliefs and practices. Some Indian Christians try to mix Christianity with traditional practices and objects that are used to worship evil spirits.

Native Christians need to see how important it is to follow the guidelines of God's Word. To help people understand this, Mr. Smith and other Christian leaders have written a book called *Boundary Lines*.

◆ ◆ ◆
Prayer
*Pray that we, as Christians, will be careful to stay away
from things that are not pleasing to God. Pray, too, that Mr.
Smith's book will be used by God for good.*

CREE

DAY ONE

One Cree Indian has written, "When God first made the earth, He made it so nice. He made good food for the animals. He made everything grow very well. He knew that the Cree people would live on this food that He put on the earth. He put in fish and He made good food for them to eat. Everything that was put here by God was beautiful."

The Creator did make all of these things. He made the heavens and the earth, and everything in them. And He said that it was good.

◆◆◆
Prayer
Thank God for making the earth and
sky, the plants and animals, and us.

DAY TWO

Traditionally, the Crees have lived in northern parts of Canada and are used to cold temperatures.

But where they live, it is so cold that the ground stays frozen much of the year. Since you can't grow crops in frozen ground, the Crees have hunted animals for food and also for furs.

They have hunted moose, elk, caribou, deer and smaller animals. They used to hunt and trap beavers, then trade the furs to French and Scottish traders. The French and the Scots would then sell the furs to people in Europe.

♦♦♦
Prayer
Thank God for making the Crees, the places where they have lived, and even the animals for them to hunt and trap.

DAY THREE

Look around you. Look outside. What do you see?

Everything around us is part of our environment—the things we see (grass, trees, and birds) and even what we don't see (dirt under the grass, water that is underground, animals that are hiding, the air we breathe). All these things are part of our environment.

The Cree people know that their environment provides what they need in order to live. They also know that the environment must be protected. They work hard to take care of the land and everything around them.

The Bible teaches that mankind should take care of the earth. It is God who has given that responsibility to us, and it is God we must worship.

◆◆◆
Prayer
*Pray that the Cree will not worship what
God has made, but worship God Himself.*

DAY FOUR

A Cree Indian has said, "Every living thing is a part of this land and was given a task to perform while living on this earth. Even the smallest living animal was given a task to contribute to this land. And the people of this land took the teachings from the land and animals."

We need to take our teachings from God's Word, not from the land and animals.

God reveals Himself to us in two ways: through what He has made and through His Word.

The Crees know about the Creator through what He has made. But they, like all people, need to hear God's Word, so they can believe in Jesus for salvation.

◆◆◆
Prayer
*Pray that the Crees will hear God's Word and
know the Creator through Jesus Christ His Son.*

DAY FIVE

On June 30, 2001, hundreds of Crees gathered to celebrate the completion of a Cree New Testament. The New Testament was translated into the James Bay dialect of Cree.

Missionaries and Cree Indians had worked on the translation for about twenty-five years.

To celebrate, they had a ceremony called "Walking Out." In this ceremony, little boys and girls, just one year old, walked out of a tepee, all dressed up in traditional Cree clothing. Holding their parents' hands, the toddlers went to find some food. Then they brought the food back to their friends and elders inside the tepee.

As one Cree said, "Our children and the New Testament in the Cree language are both venturing forth into the wider world of the Cree Nation...."

♦ ♦ ♦

Prayer

Praise God for making Himself known to the Crees through His Word. Pray that many more Crees will read the New Testament in their own language.

IROQUOIS

DAY ONE

Many Indian tribes used to live near the south side of Lake Ontario in what is now New York State.

Several of the tribes thought of themselves as an extended family. But each of these tribes lived as extended families, too. Each extended family consisted of a mother, her daughters, their husbands and children. And each extended family lived in a long building covered with bark. These buildings were called longhouses.

To keep their longhouses warm, within the extended family each nuclear family (mother, father and children) tended a fire. The fires in a longhouse formed a line down the center of the longhouse.

In the same way that the fires in their longhouses made lines, so the tribes of the Iroquois (EER-uh-kwoy) Confederation made a kind of line—from the Mohawk on the east, through the Oneida (o-NY-duh), Onondaga (on-en-DAW-guh), and Cayuga (ky-YOO-guh), all the way to the Seneca at the far west.

All of these tribes, together, formed a League of Nations called the Haudanosaunee (hawd'n-oh-SAW-nee), which means the "People of the Longhouse."

◆◆◆
Prayer
Pray that the Iroquois will come
together to worship the Heavenly Father.

DAY TWO

Because the Iroquois were united, they were stronger than they would have been as separate tribes.

As a confederation, they needed some way to govern themselves. They developed the idea of a Grand Council. One chief from each tribe would go to the Grand Council to help make decisions for the whole confederation.

Benjamin Franklin and George Washington thought a Grand Council was a great idea. They thought that maybe the different states in North America could unite as one and become the United States. Maybe each state could send a representatives to a congress to make decisions for the confederation.

It was such a great idea that they did exactly that!

♦♦♦
Prayer
Pray that the Iroquois will be united
in the Body of Christ, the Church.

Joseph Brant

DAY THREE

Women were important in Iroquois communities. They owned the houses. They raised and stored the crops. They raised the children. They cared for the elderly. They also chose the chiefs who would represent them at the Grand Council.

Women could impeach chiefs they didn't like.

All treaties had to be approved by three-fourths of all the mothers. Women could also speak in council meetings and could tell men not to go to war.

Brothers were expected to help their sisters; and men who mistreated women were punished.

◆◆◆
Prayer
Pray for unity and harmony in the marriages of the Iroquois. Pray that Iroquois men and women will submit themselves to God and follow Him.

DAY FOUR

Iroquois Indians invented a sport that the French explorers called *lacrosse*.

In this sport, players carry sticks in their hands. Each stick has a pouch on one end to hold the ball. The players must use their sticks to catch, carry and throw the ball. The object of the game is to toss the ball between two posts.

Other tribes, like the Choctaw, liked to play lacrosse, too. Games with hundreds of players were sometimes held between villages.

The games were rough. Many players were injured, and some would even die. Playing lacrosse was a way for the Indians to practice for war.

♦♦♦
Prayer
Pray that when Iroquois come together for recreation, it will be a time that is helpful for them, not harmful.

DAY FIVE

One day, a white American met a Native American. The white man was surprised to see a "real live Indian"! He didn't know they still existed. He thought all the Indians had been killed...like in the movies.

White Americans need to meet real, live Indians. And real, live Indians need to meet real, live Christians.

Many white Americans do not believe in a Creator. One Iroquois from the Mohawk tribe said, "I think there was a big mistake made (when) they removed the Creator from their life."

♦♦♦
Prayer
Pray that white Americans who do believe in the Creator, and who have put their faith in Jesus as their Savior, will introduce themselves and, more importantly, Jesus to the Iroquois people.

ONEIDA

DAY ONE

The Oneida people are one of the Iroquois tribes.

In 1766, a Christian missionary named Samuel Kirkland went to live among the Oneida. He told them about Jesus.

Chief Oskanondonha believed the Gospel message. After the Chief became a Christian, his life changed. He was more kind, and he had hope in his heart. He became known as "the white man's friend."

Together, Chief Oskanondonha and Samuel Kirkland were able to persuade the Oneida to fight alongside the American colonists during the American Revolutionary War.

◆◆◆
Prayer
Pray that many more Oneida will know the One who looks at the heart and who changes hearts.

DAY TWO

Before the American Revolution, there were other wars going on in North America. Between 1689 and 1763, the French and the British fought each other a lot. They got the Indians involved in their battles, too. These are now called the French and Indian Wars.

Most of the Iroquois fought with the British against the French in the French and Indian Wars. They also fought with the British against the American colonists in the Revolutionary War. The Iroquois were feared and highly respected as warriors.

As we know, the Oneidas were part of the Iroquois League. So when they decided to help the American colonists against the British, it was a very big decision! It meant all the other Iroquois tribes would be against them.

The Oneidas' decision was one of the most important events in the Revolutionary War!

◆◆◆
Prayer
Pray that the Oneida people will decide
to follow Christ no matter what!

DAY THREE

The Oneidas made a difference in several Revolutionary War battles, especially the Battle of Saratoga.

On August 6, 1777, a group of British soldiers was trying to march from the Great Lakes to join with General Burgoyne's army that was marching south from Canada. If the two armies could join together, they would be able to divide the colonists in two and perhaps win the war.

However, a band of colonial soldiers, together with a large group of Oneida warriors, stopped the first British group. Because the British were not able to join with General Burgoyne, Burgoyne was defeated.

After that, the French decided to help the Americans. This made a huge difference in the war!

◆◆◆
Prayer
Pray that God will use Oneida
Christians to make a difference in the world today.

DAY FOUR

During the harsh winter of 1777-1778, George Washington's troops were freezing and starving in Valley Forge. They were very discouraged.

Several Oneida Indians led by Chief Oskanondonha carried 600 bushels of corn to feed Washington's men.

An Oneida woman, named Polly, taught the Americans how to prepare the corn. When Polly refused to accept money for what she did, Martha Washington gave her a shawl and bonnet.

The shawl is still a treasure among the Oneida people.

◆ ◆ ◆
Prayer
Pray that Oneida Christians will continue to store up treasures in heaven as they give of what God has given them.

DAY FIVE

When New York state opened its land to settlers, it meant less land for the Oneidas. Some Oneidas stayed in New York, but many had to leave. One band of Oneidas purchased land on the Thames River in Ontario, Canada.

Although they had to purchase land elsewhere, the Oneidas were not paid fairly for the land which they left. The Oneida Nation is still trying to come to an agreement with the state of New York and local governments regarding the land. With the help of lawyers, they are asking for a fair solution.

Beginning in the 1820s, hundreds of Oneidas moved to Wisconsin. Many of them were Christians.

The Constitution of the Oneida Tribe of Wisconsin opens with these words: "We, the people of the Oneida Tribe of Indians of Wisconsin, grateful to Almighty God for His fostering care . . ."

◆◆◆
Prayer

Thank God for the Oneidas, and for His care for them. Pray that they will be treated fairly by the U.S. government and by state and local governments.

HURON & OTTAWA

DAY ONE

The Hurons (also known as the Wyandots) and the Ottawas were trading partners.

The Ottawas provided the Hurons with beaver furs. The Hurons, in turn, traded the furs with the French. In exchange, the French gave the Hurons cloth, glass beads, paints, metal kettles, knives and hatchets.

From 1616 to 1649, the Huron tribe played a very big part in the fur trading business.

◆◆◆
Prayer
Pray that the Hurons and Ottawas will
receive all that Jesus wants to give them.

DAY TWO

A trading business requires some type of transportation. The goods that are traded have to get from one place to another.

Back in the 1600s, there were no cars, trucks, railroads, or airplanes. Instead, people used boats to transport goods. Rivers were like roads for the boats.

The Ottawa River, located between the provinces of Quebec and Ontario, Canada, was one river that made the fur trade possible. The Ottawa flows into the St. Lawrence, and the St. Lawrence connects the Great Lakes with the Gulf of St. Lawrence. The Gulf of St. Lawrence is off the Atlantic Ocean.

At one time, the Ottawa River probably had more canoes on it than any other river in history.

◆ ◆ ◆

Prayer

Pray that the Huron and Ottawa peoples will
let Jesus guide them down the river of life.

DAY THREE

Because of the trading relationship that the Hurons had with the French, they trusted French people. The Hurons welcomed French Christian missionaries and listened to the message they brought.

In 1648, the Iroquois attacked the Hurons. The Iroquois also captured some French missionaries and burned some of them at the stake.

By 1649, the Iroquois defeated the Hurons, causing them to move to different areas. Some Hurons moved to Michigan, Wisconsin, Illinois, and Ohio.

After the defeat of the Hurons, the Ottawas traded directly with the French.

In 1660, the Iroquois attacked and defeated the Ottawas as well. The Ottawas moved west and south, to Kansas and Oklahoma.

◆ ◆ ◆

Prayer

Pray that the Hurons and Ottawas will know God's peace.

DAY FOUR

Both the Hurons and the Ottawas fought with the French against the British in the French and Indian Wars.

The French lost important battles and cities to the British.

In 1763, the French surrendered many of their American lands to the British in the Treaty of Paris.

An Ottawa Chief named Pontiac, however, would not surrender so easily. Chief Pontiac gathered other tribes together and began what is now called "Pontiac's Rebellion." He wanted to drive the British out of the Great Lakes, and he almost did. The Indians took many British forts, but they could not take Fort Pitt or Fort Detroit.

Finally, most of the Indian warriors got too tired of fighting and the British won.

♦ ♦ ♦
Prayer
Pray that the Hurons and Ottawas will be refreshed by Jesus, who gives living water.

Chief Pontiac

DAY FIVE

Because the Hurons and the Ottawas moved from Canada to the United States, they were no longer located near the French missionaries. But other Christian missionaries shared the gospel with them.

Jotham and Eleanor Meeker were missionaries to the Ottawa people in Kansas. Because of the Meekers' obvious and real love for them, many Ottawa leaders accepted Jesus as their Savior. The Meekers also helped the Indians to recover from serious illnesses. The Meekers helped provide an excellent example of how whites and Indians should respect and love one another.

About twelve years after the Meekers died, the Ottawas were forced to move to Oklahoma. There are about 10,000 Ottawas living today. Most live in Oklahoma, Michigan, and Ontario, Canada. Some of the Hurons live on reservations in Oklahoma and Kansas. Others live in Quebec.

◆◆◆

Prayer

Pray that Huron and Ottawa Christians
will let the love of Jesus flow through them.

WEEK 17

POTAWATOMI

DAY ONE

Some families enjoy camping in the summer time. Maybe your family does. Do you like being outdoors hiking or fishing or maybe even hunting? There's something about fresh air and exercise that makes food taste really good. And if it's food you picked or caught yourself, it's even better.

The Potawatomi (pot-uh-WOT-uh-me) Indians were hunters and fishermen who lived near Lake Michigan. They didn't go to the lake shore for just a couple of weeks during the summer. They stayed there all year and moved many times as the seasons changed.

The Potawatomi are closely related to the Chippewa and Ottawa tribes. They are all part of the Algonquian group of Indians.

♦♦♦
Prayer
Thank God for this world He has made—just a preview of what Jesus is preparing for us.

DAY TWO

If you had a cabin by a lake, how would you feel if you couldn't use it anymore? What if someone from another country built a shopping mall there instead?

Of course, you would still have food to eat even if you couldn't go to the lake. But what if they somehow took a few months' worth of food, too?

The Potawatomi needed the land and the food they got from it. They fought in wars to try to keep white settlers off the land.

Settlers are people who settle. Many whites permanently settled on the land. That meant the Indians couldn't use it anymore.

♦ ♦ ♦
Prayer

Pray that Christians, Indian and non Indian, will know what to do about wrong things of the past. Pray that more people will be ready for the future, to be with Jesus permanently in heaven.

DAY THREE

In the French and Indian Wars, the Potawatomi tribe sided with the French against the British. They fought against the British again in Pontiac's Rebellion. During the American Revolution, they joined with the British in fighting against the American colonists. The Potawatomis also joined with other tribes, like the Miami and Shawnee, in their wars against white settlers.

The Potawatomis were defeated in all of these wars. After being defeated so many times, they finally moved to other areas, away from white settlers.

The Potawatomis have lived in Michigan, Wisconsin, Indiana, Illinois, Iowa, Missouri, Kansas and Oklahoma, as well as Mexico and Ontario, Canada. Without their traditional homelands, they have struggled to find places to live and ways to earn a living.

◆◆◆
Prayer
Pray that Potawatomi Indians will find ways to earn a living today, and that they will know Jesus as their Life.

DAY FOUR

Some Potawatomi, Chippewa and Ottawa Indians participated in the Grand Medicine Society. This was a secret society. Their goal was to make contact with evil spirits.

In the 1880s, members of this secret society helped to develop the Big Drum Religion, also known as the Drum Dance. Indians would dance for hours to the beat of a special drum, until they literally weren't thinking straight anymore. They were delirious.

God doesn't intend people to stop thinking clearly in order to know the truth. He wants us to know and love Him with our hearts and minds.

◆◆◆
Prayer
Pray that the Potawatomis will know Jesus, the Truth, and that He will set them free from evil spirits.

DAY FIVE

Today there are seven Potawatomi groups. Altogether, they have about 28,000 members.

The Citizen band in Oklahoma is the largest group of Potawatomis, with more than 18,000 members. This band has more Christians than any other group of Potawatomis.

Jim Thorpe was a Native American athlete. He was mostly Sac Indian, with Potawatomi, Fox, Kickapoo, Menominee, French and Irish ancestry as well. He is considered by many to be one of the greatest athletes of all time. His Indian name was Bright Path.

◆◆◆
Prayer
Pray that Christian Potawatomis will tell others about Jesus, the true Bright Path to God.

MIAMI & SHAWNEE

DAY ONE

After the Revolutionary War, more white settlers moved west. This meant the Indians couldn't move around as much as they had before.

The Miami and Shawnee tribes fought against whites to protect their homelands.

In the 1790s, a Miami Indian named Little Turtle led several Indian nations to fight against the whites. After years of fighting, Little Turtle and the other chiefs surrendered. They gave up much of their territory to the whites, including large parts of what are now Ohio and Indiana.

Although he surrendered, Little Turtle is considered one of the greatest military leaders of all time.

♦♦♦
Prayer
Pray that members of the Miami, Shawnee and other Indian tribes will surrender themselves to Jesus Christ, who has all authority and power for time and eternity.

DAY TWO

Two Shawnee brothers became the leaders of their people. One was Tenskwatawa, a medicine man; the other was Tecumseh.

Tenskwatawa told Indians that they should live the way their tribes had lived for centuries. He said that whites were children of an evil spirit, and he told Indians to give up the ways of the whites, including alcohol and Christianity.

Tenskwatawa accused Delaware and Wyandot (or Huron) Christians of being witches and had them burned to death. He claimed to have special magic to fight whites.

William Harrison, governor of Indiana, ordered troops to attack and burn Tenskwatawa's village.

♦♦♦
Prayer
Pray that the Miami, Shawnee and other Indians
will not listen to any counsel that is against
the Lord God or against Jesus the Messiah.

Tecumseh

DAY THREE

Tenskwatawa's older brother, Tecumseh, traveled from village to village, giving speeches. He said to his fellow Indians, "Hear me! A single twig breaks, but a bundle of twigs is strong."

Tecumseh was trying to convince the Indians to unite against the whites. He wanted to keep whites from taking land away from the Indians.

Tecumseh led the Indians in a war that whites called Tecumseh's Rebellion, but Tecumseh's men were not able to defeat the whites.

Later, in 1813, Tecumseh was killed while fighting for the British in a battle against the Americans. The American leader in that battle was William Harrison.

◆◆◆

Prayer

Pray that the Miami, Shawnee and other Indians will be united with God through Jesus Christ.

DAY FOUR

Tenskwatawa was angry! Whites had taken land, broken treaties, burned his village, and killed his people. He spoke a curse against William Harrison.

The curse declared that Harrison would become president of the United States, but would die in office, meaning while he was still president. The other part of the curse was that every president elected in a year ending with a zero would die in office.

Harrison was elected in 1840. He died one month after becoming president. Since then, every president elected in a zero year has died in office, except President Reagan. In 1981, Reagan was shot, but not killed.

Why did President Reagan live? In 1980, Christians fasted and prayed that the curse would be broken. Also, a Christian who was a direct descendent of both President Harrison and Shawnee Indians, asked forgiveness for the "sins of [his] fathers." Other Christians repented, on behalf of our nation, for "rebelliousness, violence and witchcraft." In response, it seems that God has broken the curse!

◆◆◆

Prayer

Praise God for victory in Jesus: victory
over every curse and over death itself!

DAY FIVE

The curse on U.S. presidents was broken in 1980, so do not be afraid!

Sometimes Satan tries to make us afraid. Sometimes terrorists try to make us afraid. Remember that Jesus has already won the victory. If we love God and belong to Him, nothing can ever separate us from Him.

"Submit therefore to God. Resist the devil and he will flee from you" (James 4:7, NASB). Pray for those in authority (1 Timothy 2:1-2). "Bless and curse not" (Romans 12:14b, NASB).

◆◆◆

Prayer

Pray that God will bless the Miami, Shawnee and other
Indians, and bring them to Himself. Pray that Christians,
whatever their color, will not be afraid, but will show
the world what it means to have faith and hope in Christ.

CHEROKEE

DAY ONE

Every society, every people group, has a culture. Culture is the way people live. It affects even how we think of ourselves.

What was the culture of the Cherokees like? How did they live?

Cherokee Indians used to live along rivers and streams. They grew crops like corn, pumpkins and sunflowers. They ate wild plants like berries and walnuts, and they also used plants for medicine. They fished in the rivers. They hunted bears and deer with bows and arrows. They hunted raccoons, rabbits, squirrels, and turkeys with blowguns.

The Cherokees always wanted the best for their relatives and their people. They would do whatever they could to help their people. This was part of their culture.

◆◆◆
Prayer
Praise God for creating people in His own image, and for letting them express creativity in their own cultures.

DAY TWO

Some say the Cherokee culture is very "advanced." This sounds like the Cherokee culture is being compared to something. A standard is something against which other things are compared or measured.

What standard would you use to measure a culture?

The Cherokees developed their own alphabet and schools, and a system of government modeled after the United States. If the fact that they acted in this way makes them "advanced," then that implies the standard is (or was) white American culture.

But what about Squanto who taught the Pilgrims how to raise corn? What about the Iroquois Confederation and the example they provided to Benjamin Franklin and George Washington? Should we say white culture is "primitive" because whites learned from the Indians?

◆◆◆

Prayer

Thank Jesus for dying in our place, because
none of us measures up to God's standard.

DAY THREE

Over 300,000 Americans are Cherokee Indians.

Groups of Cherokees live in Oklahoma, North and South Carolina, Missouri, Georgia, Alabama and Tennessee. Many others live in cities such as Tulsa and Oklahoma City. They have blended into the rest of society.

When people of one culture blend in with the people of another culture so that they become like the people of the other culture, we say that they have assimilated.

Sometimes people choose to assimilate. Sometimes they are forced to assimilate. Maybe sometimes it's a little of both. They might "choose" to assimilate because they don't see any other choice.

♦ ♦ ♦

Prayer

*Pray that Christians will be sensitive to
people whose culture is different from theirs.*

DAY FOUR

George Washington promised that the United States would protect the Cherokees and their lands. But later, the U.S. government did not keep the promise that Washington had made.

White settlers wanted the land where the Cherokees lived. It did not matter that the Cherokees were "civilized," that they had built house, established farms, and had become Christians. The whites wanted their land and houses. They wanted the

83

farms. They especially wanted the land once someone discovered gold in it!

The United States not only stopped protecting Cherokee land, but eventually forced the tribe to leave their homeland and go to Oklahoma.

About 4,000 Cherokees, more than one-fourth of their population at the time, died on the "Trail of Tears."

♦♦♦
Prayer
Pray that God will help us to
look past culture to hurting hearts.

DAY FIVE

Culture has to do with how people live and think. A certain culture belongs to a certain people group. Christianity has to do with how people live and think. Does Christianity belong to a certain people group? Does it belong to those who have a certain culture?

No. Christians belong to Christ. And Christ belongs to Christians. If Christ belongs to us and we belong to Him, He will show us how to live and think, because He lives in us. He will show us what changes need to be made in our own lives and in our own culture.

Today, many Cherokees belong to Christ. Many are helping others to know Him, too. They know that Jesus is not just for people of one culture, but for people of all cultures. They know that belonging to Jesus is not just for now, but for eternity.

♦♦♦
Prayer
Praise God that in heaven there will be people from every
tribe, language, people group and nation. They will all belong
to Jesus because He purchased them with His blood!

CHICKASAW

DAY ONE

The young Chickasaw woman carefully prepared her corn, making a special food called hominy. She smiled as she recalled what an older Chickasaw woman had told her the night before. When the hominy was finished, she put it in a bowl and placed the bowl in front of her house.

It wasn't long before the older woman's nephew came and noticed the bowl of hominy. He asked the young woman if he could have her permission to eat it. She said yes. By answering yes, she had just accepted the young man's proposal of marriage.

Marriage was important to American Indians. And so were the roles of men and women. Indian children learned from an early age that men and women had different roles. Men did the hunting and fishing, and they were the warriors. Women raised the young children, cooked the food and made the clothes.

♦♦♦
Prayer
Pray that Chickasaw husbands and wives
will let Christ be the head of their homes.

DAY TWO

The Chickasaws were respected as warriors. They were attacked many times by the French, but the French could not conquer them.

Native Americans took warfare very seriously. They would prepare for war by playing games like lacrosse. Playing lacrosse helped them learn to move quickly to accomplish their purpose.

Before a tribe would declare war, the tribal elders would meet with the chief to discuss the situation. They had to agree together before they would go to war.

When they won a battle, they would celebrate the victory for days. Victory probably made the men feel strong and confident in their ability to defend their families.

♦♦♦
Prayer
Pray that Chickasaw men will be strong in Christ, and be respected by their families.

DAY THREE

The Chickasaws, like many Indians, were very hospitable. They would share the last of their food with other members of their tribe. Of course, if enemies threatened the tribe, the Chickasaws would fight before they would offer food to the invaders.

In 1540, Spanish explorer Hernando de Soto became the first European to meet the Chickasaw people. In spite of

Chickasaw arrows, de Soto and his men brought rafts of soldiers, swords and horses across the Tombigbee River.

The Spaniards stayed through the winter and persuaded Chickasaw chiefs to give them food. In the spring, de Soto demanded that 200 Chickasaw men carry his equipment for him. In response, Chickasaw warriors added fire to their arrows and attacked the invaders.

Flames whipped through the houses that the Spaniards had taken from the Chickasaws. De Soto and the other Spaniards who managed to escape the fires stayed briefly in another village. They made new clothes, tried to fix some of their belongings, and then left!

◆◆◆
Prayer
Pray that many Chickasaws will welcome Christ
into their hearts, knowing they can trust Him.

Day Four

The Chickasaws lived close to the Mississippi River, in northern Mississippi, and parts of Tennessee, Arkansas and Kentucky. Some of them decided to move west before the 1830s.

Those who stayed near the Mississippi were later forced to move to Oklahoma. The Chickasaws were one of the five "Civilized Tribes" of the Southeast. Like the Cherokee, Choctaw, Creek and Seminole tribes, the Chickasaws also experienced the terrible tragedy of the "Trail of Tears."

◆◆◆
Prayer
Pray that Chickasaw families will realize that Christ
laid down His life for His bride, and that He is asking
them to be part of His bride by putting their trust in Him.

DAY FIVE

The "Trail of Tears" was a horrible injustice. But today it is more than dead facts written in history books; it is pain written in the hearts of many Native Americans.

Wounds in a nation can easily lead to wounds in families. Just as it is hard for injured warriors to fight, it is hard for wounded hearts to be strong.

Hopelessness has found a home in many Indian hearts. As a result, Indians often struggle with weak marriages and poor families.

Leaders among the Chickasaw and other Indian nations are trying to find ways to help Indian fathers to become strong leaders within their families. These fathers need to know that Christians care... and that Jesus cares.

◆ ◆ ◆
Prayer
Pray that Chickasaw families will let Jesus give them hope and make them whole, holy, and strong.

OSAGE

DAY ONE

Pronouncing words in another language is not always easy. Back in 1673, a French explorer named Marquette tried to pronounce Wazhazhe. It was the name of an Indian tribe. He could not get the name right, and ever since then, the tribe has been called the Osage (o-SAYJ).

The Osage were related to other tribes like the Omaha, Kaw, Ponca, Kansa and Quapaw. These tribes spoke similar languages because they were originally one group of people.

The Osages lived mostly along rivers in Missouri, Arkansas, and Kansas. This area is part of the Great Plains. On the Great Plains, there is wide open land where you can see for long distances.

♦♦♦
Prayer
Pray that the Osages will rejoice that the Creator of the universe knows their name and everything about them.

DAY TWO

The Osages had a special council of elderly men called the Little Old Men. This council was part of the tribe's political system. They made laws and settled disputes.

Every people group has its own social system: how members relate to each other. The Osage people were divided into different clans. Each clan had something special to do in order to help the whole tribe.

In the religious system of the Osages, priests were supposed to figure out the universe and explain it to the rest of the people.

The Osages believed that the way their political, social, and religious systems worked together was similar to how different parts of the universe, or cosmos, work together. They tried hard to understand the cosmos.

♦ ♦ ♦
Prayer
Pray that the Osage will realize that the Creator of the universe has taken the initiative to communicate with them!

DAY THREE

For most of the year, the Osages lived in permanent villages. They grew corn and squash.

During other times of the year, they went on long buffalo hunts. During hunting season, they lived in tepees. The tepees could be packed up and moved quickly, making it easier for the Indians to follow the buffalo herds.

The Osages were some of the first Indians to get guns and horses from the Europeans. Guns and horses made it much easier to hunt buffalo.

♦♦♦
Prayer

Pray that the Osages will receive the simple message of the gospel... —just what they need in their hunt for understanding the Creator.

DAY FOUR

Each Osage village had two chiefs: a peace chief and a war chief.

Osage warriors were fierce. In earlier times, they used clubs, hatchets, and tomahawks as weapons. When they got guns, they had an advantage over other tribes. The Osage were enemies of many tribes.

Like other Indians, they would take the scalps of their enemies to show as proof of their courage.

Another custom of the Osage and other Indians was to paint their faces and bodies before going to war. They did this to try to make their enemies afraid. But deep down, they had fears of their own. They wanted spiritual protection, and they thought war paint would somehow give it to them.

♦♦♦
Prayer

Pray that the Osage people will know they can have spiritual protection and be forever free from fear through the blood of Jesus Christ, the Son of the Creator.

DAY FIVE

In 1802, the French persuaded the Osages to go and settle where Oklahoma is today. The Osages had always fiercely protected their homeland. Yet, at the same time, they tried to think about what would be best in the future. Would Oklahoma be better for them?

Some decided yes. They became some of the first Indians to arrive in Oklahoma. Eventually, other Indian tribes were sent there, too. It wasn't easy for so many tribes to live in such a small area.

Fortunately, what you see on the land is not all there is. Deep in the ground, beneath the Osage people of Oklahoma, huge quantities of oil and gas were discovered. Since 1897, the Osage reservation has received over $1 billion from oil and gas.

There are over 18,000 Osages today. Their capitol is in Pawhuska, Oklahoma.

◆ ◆ ◆
Prayer
*Pray that many Osages will soon enjoy
the priceless treasure of knowing the Creator,
through Jesus Christ.*

CROW

DAY ONE

Parenting was important to the Crow Indians. Fathers trained their sons in skills like archery and war. Mothers trained their daughters to cook and make clothing.

Parents would praise their children for improvements they were making. When a boy returned from fighting in his first war, members of his father's clan would surround him, sing songs, and offer prayers for him.

One relative, called the "joking relative," would make fun of the boy's behavior...in a friendly way.

◆◆◆
Prayer
Pray that Crow Indians, young and old alike,
will know God as their Father.

DAY TWO

The Crows used to be part of the Hidatsa tribe. But sometime in the 1700s, they split off and moved west into Wyoming and Montana.

When the Crows moved away from the Hidatsas, their lives changed. They stopped growing crops except for tobacco. They stopped making pottery. And they stopped living in permanent villages.

Instead, they became buffalo hunters who lived in portable tepees. They learned to gather and eat wild foods.

◆ ◆ ◆
Prayer

*Pray that the Crows will become children
of God, and let Him change their lives!*

DAY THREE

The Crows wanted to know God. They tried different ways
to find Him. But in their search, they wound up communicating
with evil spirits. They didn't know that the spirits were not of
God and would not lead them to God.

They used drugs, did dances, fasted, and sweated in sweat
lodges. They wanted to have visions or dreams because they
wanted the spirits to communicate with them and help them
make important decisions.

When a Crow young man was preparing to be a hunter, he
would go away from the tribe and fast for several days. He did
this because he was seeking a vision.

The young man would remember the first animal he saw in
his vision. He believed this animal would be his protector for
the rest of his life. After that, for the rest of his days, he would
never kill an animal of that species.

◆ ◆ ◆
Prayer

*Pray that Crow Indians will come under
the authority and protection of the Heavenly
Father through Jesus Christ His Son.*

DAY FOUR

Today, there are more than 10,000 Crow Indians. Most of
them live on a reservation in southern Montana.

Crow families usually do not make very much money.

Many of the adults don't have jobs, and many of them have never finished high school. These are problems that other Indian tribes face, too.

Many Native American young people suffer from abuse, depression, and hopelessness. They have no hope for their future.

It is hard for Indian children to handle the pressures that they face. They often feel pressured to go back to the ways of their ancestors and worship false gods. At the same time, they feel pressured to be like other Americans and watch sinful things on videos or television, or to look at Internet web sites that are not pleasing to God.

♦♦♦
Prayer
Pray that Indian young people
will choose to follow Christ
Who understands everything
that they and their people have
ever experienced.

Sits-in-the-Middle
of the Land

DAY FIVE

A Native American young person in Montana describes his people. He writes:

The neediest group of people in the country are the Native Americans. . . . My people see no future. . . . [T]he one group that could help them, Christians, ignores my people.

Every summer, thousands of Anglo teenagers embark on mission experiences to Mexico, the Caribbean, South America, Eastern Europe, the Far East, Africa and the Philippines. How many . . . are willing to . . . go to a place filled with extreme poverty . . . high unemployment and hopelessness . . . a place practically in their own backyard? . . .

Please, Christian America, give my people Jesus and His values—the only hope of my people.[1]

◆◆◆
Prayer
Pray that Christian young people across America will reach out in love and share the good news of Jesus with those who live in our midst.

---

[1] Used by permission of Ron Hutchcraft Ministries, Inc. www.gospelcom.net/rhm/eagles/vision.htm.

SIOUX

DAY ONE

"Oh, give me a home where the buffalo roam. . . . " The place where the buffalo roamed was the home of many Indian tribes, including the Lakota Sioux. The deer and the antelope played there, too, running through the lush grass of the Great Plains.

The Lakota Sioux were one branch of the Sioux Indians. There were three other main branches: the Dakota, the Yankton Nakota, and the Yanktonai Nakota.

When the Ojibwa/Chippewa tribe forced the Sioux to migrate south and west, the Lakotas moved west to the Black Hills. The Nakotas made their home along the Missouri River; the Yanktonai Nakotas went to the area that we now call the Dakotas; and the Dakota Sioux stayed along the Minnesota River in Minnesota.

♦♦♦

Prayer

Pray that members of all of these groups
will become members of the Body of Christ
and contribute their gifts to the rest of the Body.

DAY TWO

Each group of Sioux Indians developed its own lifestyle based on the place where it lived. The Lakotas hunted buffalo and lived in tepees.

Other tribes also moved to the plains to hunt buffalo.

During the 1800s, millions of buffalo lived on the Great Plains.

For the Lakotas and other Plains Indians, buffalo became their most important source of food, clothing and many other things they needed.

The buffalo herds migrated northwest in the spring and southeast in the fall. When the buffalo moved, the Indians moved. If necessary, the Indians would move several times a month.

♦♦♦
Prayer
Pray that more Sioux will abide in Christ, letting Him provide all they need for a lifestyle of obedience to Him.

DAY THREE

The Plains Indians learned many different ways to use meat from the buffalo. They dried strips of meat to make jerky. Drying preserved the meat and made it easy for the Indians to store and carry it with them.

They also ground dried meat into a powder called pemmican (PEM-ih-ken). This meat powder was a high-energy food that could last for years. The Indians would mix it with fat and berries, or put it into sausage.

Buffalo hides were used for clothing and tepees. Horns and bones were used for tools. Buffalo hair was woven into ropes, and tails were used as fly swatters.

♦♦♦
Prayer
Thank God for providing the Indians with buffalo to meet so many of their needs. Pray that Indians will trust God to meet all of their needs forever in Jesus Christ, His Son.

DAY FOUR

When the buffalo herd moved, the Lakota Sioux could pack up an entire camp of six hundred tepees in just a few minutes. At the signal of the chief, they would take down every tepee, load their horses and dogs, and be on their way.

The chief would select the location for the next campsite. He always looked for a spot that had plenty of good grass for the horses and water for everyone. And, of course, it had to be near buffalo!

The Lakotas arranged their tepees according to family relationships. Newlyweds put up their tepees close to one set of parents.

◆ ◆ ◆
Prayer
Pray that the Sioux will trust the Father to lead them. He knows what lies ahead.

Chief Sitting Bull

DAY FIVE

In the summer, when the berries were ripe, different clans of Sioux would come together for a special event, the Sun Dance. The purpose of the Sun Dance was to give thanks and to ask the Great Spirit for a renewal of nature, for healing of the sick, for victory in battle, for success in marriages, and for the settlement of quarrels.

The entire Sun Dance ceremony lasted twelve days. For the

first few days, the Indians would visit with each other, tell stories, smoke tobacco, race horses, and compete in games.

Then they became more serious. They danced, sang songs and pounded drums. Toward the end of the celebration, the bravest ones would cut skin from their bodies. Some would poke a skewer in their skin and use it to fasten themselves to a pole.

Those who suffered and hung from a pole believed that their suffering would bring them special blessings and even help the whole tribe.

◆◆◆

Prayer

Pray that the Sioux who know Jesus will bless others by telling them that Jesus is the only One who could suffer and die to save us; that He did this on the cross; and that He rose again victorious.

BLACKFEET

DAY ONE

A group of Indians was traveling to meet some other Indians. On the way to their destination, they happened to walk over some burned prairie land. When the group reached their destination, their feet were black with soot. That's how they became known as "Blackfeet."

The Blackfeet roamed along what is now the American-Canadian border, where Alberta and Montana meet. They were hunters who followed the buffalo herds.

Now the huge buffalo herds are gone, and the Blackfeet have a reservation in northwest Montana.

◆◆◆
Prayer
Pray that the Blackfeet will bow their knees
to the One Whose Name is above all names.

DAY TWO

How did the Blackfeet get their buffalo? Before the days of horses and guns, Indians would try to sneak up on the buffalo. They would hide in the prairie grass, and sometimes even dress in animal skins to look like animals. Then they would slowly creep into the buffalo herds and shoot their arrows.

Indians sometimes frightened the animals to cause them to run over cliffs and fall to their deaths. When they could do that, it was a big day for the buffalo hunters.

Later, when they began to use horses, the Indians no longer needed to disguise themselves. Instead they would ride into the herd on horseback. They would then guide their horses to run beside the running buffalo and shoot their arrows. One the Indians owned guns, shooting buffalo became even easier.

◆ ◆ ◆
Prayer
Pray that the Blackfeet will wait on God and be renewed in Jesus—that they might run in His strength and not be weary.

DAY THREE

Blackfeet warriors stole horses from the Spanish in 1787. They also stole horses from other Indian tribes.

Sometimes the different Indian tribes fought each other. When the Europeans came, it meant even more groups were present to fight each other. Eventually, the United States, Canada and Mexico became independent countries and they, too, began to fight—against the Indians, against the Europeans, and even against one another.

All kinds of wars were fought between these different tribes, peoples and nations in North America. Sometimes the members of one group would kill members of another just to get even for something the other had done.

102

In the 1860s, Blackfeet Indians began attacking white settlers. When an Indian chief's brother was killed, a Blackfeet warrior killed a white man. United States soldiers then killed 200 Blackfeet. . . .

♦♦♦

Prayer

Pray that the Blackfeet will surrender to Jesus
and let Him embrace them in His loving arms.

DAY FOUR

What happened to the buffalo? White men, called "hide hunters," killed a lot of buffaloes to make money. Buffalo hides were used for coats and leather; bones were used for fertilizer. A lot of buffalo meat, however, was left to rot on the plains.

The United States government wanted Indians to move to reservations. The Indians, of course, didn't want to change their way of life. They wanted to roam around on the wide open land, following the buffalo.

The U.S. government realized that if the buffalo were gone, the Indians would have to change their lifestyle. Without any buffaloes, Indians on the Great Plains would need help from the government in order to survive. Then, it would be easier to persuade them to live on reservations.

So the government established policies that encouraged hunters to destroy as many buffaloes as possible.

By 1886, only 541 buffalo were left.

♦♦♦

Prayer

Pray that the Blackfeet will forgive whites for killing
the buffaloes and taking their land, and that the hearts and
minds of the Blackfeet will be set free in Christ.

DAY FIVE

When the Blackfeet and other Plains Indians lost the buffalo herds, they lost their food, clothing, tepees, tools, and their entire way of life. They went to live on reservations and became dependent on the United States government for food and supplies.

The Blackfeet were once called the "Lords of the Plains." Since being forced to live on reservations, they have struggled to learn new ways of living. Some have raised livestock. In recent years, natural resources like oil, gas and coal have been of some help.

One Blackfeet legend says that the Creator, called Old Man, made all things and taught the Indians how to use them. He told them, "I will always take care of you, and someday I will return."

◆ ◆ ◆
Prayer
Pray that the Blackfeet will give themselves completely to Jesus, the Son of the Creator, the King of kings, the One who will return for His people someday.

CHEYENNE

DAY ONE

The Cheyenne are "beautiful people." That's what their name means. Other tribes respected them for their height, intelligence and courage.

The Cheyenne moved south from Minnesota, then west to the Dakotas, where they settled along the Missouri River. Later they moved to the Black Hills. From there, the Sioux pushed them further south.

Eventually they settled along the Platte River in Wyoming and Nebraska. The Cheyenne who stayed along the Platte River became the Northern Cheyenne. The Southern Cheyenne were those who went to live along the Arkansas River in Colorado and Kansas.

◆◆◆
Prayer
Thank God for the Cheyenne people whom
He created in His image, for His glory.

DAY TWO

It was important for a young Cheyenne woman to stay pure and wait for the man who would be her husband. The young man had some waiting to do, too. If a man wanted to marry a woman, he had to court her first. Courting could last five years.

Before a courtship began, a young brave would wait day after day near the path, hoping a particular young lady would talk to him. He might whistle and call out to her, and even tug at her robe. If she liked him, she could choose to talk to him. If not, she could ignore him.

If she did respond, and if both of their families approved,

then the courtship could begin. In order to prove he was serious, the man's family would offer gifts to the young lady's family.

Finally, the couple could marry.

♦♦♦
Prayer
Pray that the Cheyenne will hear Jesus calling them and respond to His great love for them.

DAY THREE

Cheyenne chiefs were expected to be wise, kind, generous, fair, and brave. They had to put other people first.

The Cheyennes were governed by a council of forty-four chiefs. Each chief governed an extended family called a band.

The chief's job was to settle disputes, decide when to move

camp, when to make agreements with other tribes, and when to go to war.

When the chiefs decided to go to war, the warriors followed their orders.

◆ ◆ ◆
Prayer
Pray that the Cheyenne will know Jesus' amazing love for them, a love so great that He died in their place.

DAY FOUR

In 1840, the Cheyennes united with other Plains Indians to resist white settlers.

One band of 600 Cheyennes, however, made a peace treaty with the United States government. The government promised to protect these Indians if they would settle near Sand Creek in Southern Colorado.

The Indians did as they were told. But a former minister, Colonel John Chivington, paid no attention to the peace treaty. Early one cold November morning in 1864, just as the Cheyenne families were beginning to wake up, Chivington and his troops rode into the village and attacked. They killed and scalped almost all of the Indians.

◆ ◆ ◆
Prayer
Ask God to show us His heart of love and compassion, especially for people groups who have been so terribly mistreated.

DAY FIVE

When Chivington's troops returned to Denver, they were not arrested for murder. Instead, a parade was held in their honor. Instead of being ashamed, the men who had participated in the raid were proud.

When people are proud, they think they are better than others. When they think they are better than others, they do not love others. Pride greatly displeases God. In fact, the Bible says that "God is opposed to the proud, but gives grace to the humble" (James 4:6b, NASB).

After the Sand Creek massacre, Indians all across the Plains rose up to defend themselves.

More than a hundred years later, President Clinton set aside thousands of acres along Sand Creek to serve as a permanent memorial to the Cheyennes.

Over 12,000 Cheyennes now live on reservations in Montana and Oklahoma. How can we show God's love to them?

◆ ◆ ◆
Prayer
Ask God to help us not be proud, but to humble ourselves before Him and let Him use us to show His love to others.

PAWNEE

DAY ONE

The Pawnees were friendly toward the whites. After the United States made the Louisiana Purchase in 1803, large numbers of white settlers moved into Pawnee territory. Yet the Pawnees helped the whites instead of fighting against them. Some Pawnees worked as guards to defend railroad construction crews against attacks from other Indian tribes. Others became scouts for the U.S. Cavalry.

They were probably hoping the whites would help them in return. The Pawnees needed help to defend themselves against the Sioux and other Indian tribes. These other tribes often raided Pawnee villages and stole their food.

◆◆◆
Prayer
*Pray that the Pawnees will look to Jesus
to be their Savior and Defender forever.*

DAY TWO

Sometimes the Pawnees went on buffalo hunts. But most of the time, they stayed in permanent villages in houses made of earth.

The Pawnees put buffalo fat in their hair. They would rub it in until their hair stuck together and pointed straight up. Then they would curve it toward the back. When they were finished, it looked like a horn. The name *Pawnee* probably comes from a description of this hair-style.

The Pawnees lived near rivers in Nebraska, Colorado, and Kansas. In 1770, the Southern Pawnee tribe joined the Skidi Pawnees in what is now known as Nebraska. There, they lived along the Platte River.

Because the Pawnees built homes and remained in one place, they were able to raise crops. Corn was their main crop. Today, farmers in Nebraska, Colorado and Kansas still use some of the same types of corn seeds that the Pawnees used.

◆◆◆
Prayer
Pray that the hearts of the Pawnee will be like good soil for the seeds of Truth.

DAY THREE

Some of the Great Plains Indian tribes fought against the whites. One way that the U.S. government tried to keep Indians from attacking was to give them gifts. Among the gifts were rifles to use in hunting buffalo. The Pawnees, who were friendly, were not given rifles.

The Sioux viewed the Pawnees as enemies because the Pawnees helped the whites. In 1873, a Sioux war party attacked a Pawnee hunting party in southern Nebraska and killed 150 Pawnees, including their chief. Without rifles, it was hard for the Pawnees to defend themselves.

In spite of their helpfulness to the whites, the Pawnees were not allowed to stay in their homeland. They were forced to live on a reservation on the Loup River in Nebraska. Eventually, however, the U.S. government persuaded them to sell the reservation and leave Nebraska.

Like many other tribes, the Pawnee headed for Oklahoma.

◆ ◆ ◆
Prayer
*Pray that the hearts of
Pawnees will be
willing to trust in Jesus.*

DAY FOUR

The Pawnee, Natchez and Aztec tribes had similar religious beliefs and practices. They all worshiped the sun, and they all had priests who were respected by the rest of the tribe.

Like the Aztec and Natchez peoples, some Pawnees also practiced human sacrifice. Once a year, they would raid another tribe to capture a young girl about 13 years of age. They would let her live among them for many months, treating her with special kindness. Then they would sacrifice her.

They believed her death would fertilize the earth so they could have greater harvests.

When people worship false gods, they try to do things that will bring good results. They try to earn favor with their gods. Even if something is evil, they may do it if they think it will please their gods and bring success.

◆ ◆ ◆
Prayer
*Pray that the Pawnees will know that they don't have to
try to earn the favor of the true God, but that they must
believe in their hearts that God raised Jesus from the dead.*

111

DAY FIVE

Deep in their hearts, people who worship evil spirits know that they do not do it because of love, but because of fear. Because of that fear, it is hard for them to stop worshipping the evil spirits.

In 1816, a young Pawnee chief had the courage to follow his conscience. Just as the priests were about to sacrifice a Comanche girl, 19-year-old Chief Petalesharo stepped up and ordered them to stop.

Other brave warriors stood with the chief against the priests. The Pawnees never again practiced human sacrifice. Today, Petalesharo is a hero to the Pawnees.

◆◆◆

Prayer

Pray that Jesus' love will replace fear in the hearts of the Pawnees; that they will let Jesus be their Lord; and that they will tell others about Jesus.

PAIUTE & UTE

DAY ONE

Have you ever been to a desert? If you have, do you remember what you ate there? The Paiute and Ute Indians didn't have supermarkets near their homes in Utah, Arizona, New Mexico, Colorado, Oregon and Nevada. Food was scarce in these dry desert and mountain areas.

In drier climates, there is less plant life, and less plant life means less animal life. That all adds up to less food.

Because their food supplies were so limited, the Paiutes and Utes lived very differently from the Indians of the forests and the Great Plains. They looked for food whenever and wherever they could find it. They had to spread out to find things to eat. As a result, the tribes were divided into different clans that lived in various locations.

Even the members of one clan were unable to stay in one place very long. They had to move often to search for food.

♦♦♦
Prayer
Pray that the Paiutes and Utes will look to God—the same God who provided for the children of Israel as they wandered in the desert—for all they need.

DAY TWO

In March, the Paiutes and Utes hunted ground squirrels and geese. In April, they used nets to catch ducks, and looked for duck eggs. In May, they went to the rivers to catch fish.

In July, they harvested rice grass and ground up the seeds. They ground roasted ants with seeds in order to make flour. They ate caterpillars and crickets, and enjoyed fresh berries. They dried roots and bulbs for the winter, and gathered herbs to use for medicines.

In September, they gathered pine nuts. At this time of year, they were still in the hills, escaping the sun-scorched desert below.

In November, they would leave the hills and return to warmer desert areas. The clans came together for rabbit hunts. They used rabbit skins to make warm clothing. Deserts get cold at night!

♦♦♦
Prayer
Pray that the Paiutes and Utes will feed on the timeless truths of the Bible, a book not authored by men, but inspired by the Holy Spirit.

DAY THREE

The Paiutes and Utes didn't spend much time building houses, since they had to move so often. Instead, they made dome-shaped wickiups (WICK-ee-ups).

A wickiup is a small house made from wooden poles covered by reeds and brush. A fire pit in the center provided warmth and a spot for cooking. A hole in the ceiling let the smoke out.

After they got horses in the 1700s, the Paiutes and Utes did hunt some buffalo. However, they didn't hunt buffalo as much as some other tribes did. One way they used the buffalo hides was to cover their wickiups.

◆ ◆ ◆

Prayer

Pray that the Paiutes and Utes will let Jesus be their shelter—the same Jesus who traveled from place to place here on earth, without a permanent home in which to lay His head.

DAY FOUR

In the late 1880s, a Paiute started a religion that spread to the Plains Indians. It was called the Ghost Dance Religion. He taught that the earth would soon be reborn. He said the buffalo and Indian ancestors would return, but all whites would be gone.

He told other Indians that if they danced this dance, they would receive visions of the future world. He taught that the Indians must live together in peace, and that they must abandon all of the white man's ways, including Christianity.

The new religion gave the Indians hope. If it was true, then they would be able to live as they had been living for hundreds of years.

♦♦♦
Prayer
*Pray that the Paiutes and Utes will
experience new birth by believing in Jesus, who
laid down His life for all the peoples of the world.*

DAY FIVE

The Lakota Sioux were among those who followed the teachings of the Paiute Indians and the Ghost Dance Religion.

As the Lakotas followed this new religion, some of their religious practices caused alarm to the whites. Because they were afraid the Lakotas might attack, the U.S. army arrested Chief Sitting Bull. One of Sitting Bull's followers shot a policeman, and the policeman shot Sitting Bull.

After Sitting Bull died, the whites were still afraid of the Indians. They rounded up Chief Big Foot and a band of Lakota Sioux at a place called Wounded Knee. There Lakota men, women and children were massacred by the whites.

The massacre affected Indians of many tribes. Their hearts were wounded, their hopes smashed.

♦♦♦
Prayer
*Pray that the Paiutes, Utes, Sioux and other Indians
will forgive. Pray that they will know that salvation through
Jesus is God's plan for them . . . and their only hope.*

PUEBLO

DAY ONE

Pueblo is not the name of just one Indian tribe. It is a description of how certain tribes lived. The Spanish used the word *Pueblo* to refer to Indians who lived in permanent villages. In fact, *Pueblo* is a Spanish word meaning village.

Today, we still use the name Pueblo. It refers to a group of Indians in the southwestern United States.

In New Mexico and eastern Arizona there are nineteen Pueblo villages that make up the "All Indian Pueblo Council." These villages work together on issues such as land and water resources, education, and culture. However, each village is part of a separate Indian nation.

◆◆◆
Prayer
Pray that Pueblo Indians will have a personal relationship with God, who laid the foundations of the earth.

DAY TWO

The Pueblo tribes came from the Anasazi Indians. Hundreds of years ago, the Anasazi built a huge building in Chaco Canyon, New Mexico. It was five stories high and contained 800 rooms. At one point, about 1,000 people lived in this building.

From 900 to 1150 AD, Chaco Canyon was a busy place. Stone-covered roads made it easier for people to get to Chaco Canyon.

For some reason, Chaco Canyon was abandoned. We don't know exactly why. We do know, however, that there was a drought in the late 1200s. People had to move in search of water.

Some of the Anasazis went to the Rio Grande area of New Mexico. They are known today as the Rio Grande Pueblo Indians. Other Anasazis went to what is now northeastern Arizona. Their descendants are the Hopis. Still others moved to western New Mexico and intermarried with other Indians. These people are called Zunis.

◆◆◆
Prayer
Pray that Pueblos will know Jesus
as their Fortress and their Deliverer.

DAY THREE

Some Pueblo Indians developed irrigation canals that brought water from rivers to their fields. This made it possible for them to raise larger crops. Pueblo farmers grew corn, beans, squash, tobacco, sunflowers, and cotton.

At one time, the Pueblos built their houses as covered pits. Later they built their homes above ground. Some of the old style buildings are still used for religious purposes. They are called kivas (KEE-vuhs).

Pueblo homes have come in different styles. One style used logs covered with mud. Another style used adobe bricks. In the third style, stones were mortared together and covered with plaster.

◆◆◆
Prayer
Pray that the Pueblos will let Jesus
be their Rock and their Refuge.

DAY FOUR

Settling down in one place, and growing large crops to feed many people, gave the Pueblos more time to make crafts. They made beautiful pottery, baskets and turquoise jewelry.

You can buy Pueblo jewelry, pottery and crafts in villages like Acoma or Taos, New Mexico. These ancient Pueblo villages have had people living in them longer than any other city in North America.

There are over 50,000 Pueblo Indians today. For many, their lifestyle is similar to the way their ancestors lived.

Of all North America native peoples, the Hopis live closest to the way their ancestors did.

◆◆◆

Prayer

*Pray that the Pueblo peoples will know
security, stability, and strength in Jesus.*

DAY FIVE

Christians have tried to force their religion on the Indians. Because of this, many reject Christianity, even though they may not understand what salvation through Jesus Christ really means.

In very old Pueblo villages, you can see mission churches that were built hundreds of years ago. Some Pueblos who attend these churches mix Christianity with their traditional religions. In some ways, they try to keep their traditional religious practices a secret. Certain religious ceremonies can only be performed in kivas.

Kiva means "underground." And while kiva buildings are literally underground, there is another meaning for the word: that is, "secretive." Their resistance to Christianity has caused many Pueblos to take their religion underground. It seems that outside pressures have caused them to hold on to their traditional beliefs and lifestyles even stronger than they would have had there been no pressures.

The Pueblo Indian governments do not allow Christian preaching or teaching on their lands.

◆ ◆ ◆
Prayer
Pray that the love of Christ will melt hardened hearts, and that many Pueblo people will be changed by the Holy Spirit from the inside out.

APACHE

DAY ONE

Not all of the tribes in the southwest lived in permanent villages. The Apaches, for example, were nomadic. They moved around, and did not stay in the same place very long. As hunters and warriors, they roamed the land that is now Arizona, Colorado, New Mexico, Kansas, Oklahoma, Texas and Mexico.

The Apaches raided the villages of other tribes. They took food from the Hopis and Zunis, and later stole horses from them, too.

The Apaches would come in quickly, take what they wanted, and leave so fast that no one could fight back.

It was the Zunis who gave them their name, *Apachu*, which means "enemy."

◆◆◆
Prayer
Pray that Apaches will know that Jesus died
for all of us even while we were still enemies of God.

DAY TWO

Have you ever seen an Apache fiddle? It's kind of like a violin, but with only one string. The Apaches made their fiddles out of the stalks of a white-flowered plant called a yucca. They used an animal tendon for the string. They played their fiddles with something like a violin bow.

Most Apaches lived in dome-shaped wickiups, but some

lived in tepees.

They hunted deer and rabbits for food and ate desert plants like cactus. Raiding other tribes brought in more food. Some Apaches grew crops, and some of the Eastern Apaches hunted buffalo. Originally they wore clothes made from deerskins. Later, they began wearing cotton and wool clothing that they got from raiding or trading with other tribes.

♦ ♦ ♦
Prayer
Pray that Apaches will realize the blessings of
God's free gift of salvation through Jesus Christ.

DAY THREE

When the Spanish came, Apaches stole horses and cattle from them.

After the Spanish, the Apaches fought the Mexicans. Some Apaches helped the Texas Militia and farmers gain independence from Mexico.

After gaining freedom from Mexico, many Apaches fought the new American government and raided white settlers. They didn't want whites passing through their territory. When white travelers came through on their way to California to search for gold, the Apaches resented them for trespassing on their land.

♦ ♦ ♦
Prayer
Pray that the Apaches will have
peace with God through Jesus Christ.

DAY FOUR

Like other Native Americans, the Apaches believed in supernatural beings. In religious dances, Apache men would try to

Geronimo

look and act like spirits. They would dress up in costumes, paint themselves, and put on masks and headdresses.

Spanish Christians tried to force the Apaches to give up these types of practices and go to mission churches. The Apaches resisted and rejected the religion of the Spaniards.

Even today many Indians resist Christianity because they think it is the religion of the white people. They need to know that Jesus came for all peoples.

♦♦♦
Prayer
*Pray that many Apaches will realize the good
news about Jesus is not about religious practices but about
knowing Jesus personally and letting Him live in us.*

DAY FIVE

Apache Indians resisted being confined to a reservation. Some fought and some ran away rather than permitting themselves to be forced onto reservations. Yet today, most Apaches do live on reservations in New Mexico and Arizona. A few live around Apache, Oklahoma.

Some of their most popular occupations include raising livestock, farming, operating sawmills and stores, making and selling crafts, and operating gambling facilities.

Other tribes besides the Apaches are involved in the gambling industry. At first, gambling seemed to bring lots of money to the Indian tribes. Unfortunately, gambling often leads to bad habits that are hard to break, broken relationships because of bad habits, and even crime.

Organized crime refers to groups who work together to plan and commit crimes. Because of gambling, organized crime has come to some Indian reservations.

♦♦♦
Prayer
*Pray that Apaches will receive the gift of God's
abundant grace, which brings righteousness and life.*

NAVAJO

Day One

Navajo (NAV-uh-ho) Indians have had an influence on world history. During World War II, the U.S. Army was looking for some kind of code that the Japanese would not be able to break.

They recruited Navajo men to be "Code Talkers." Navajo soldiers would translate English messages into Navajo and send the messages to other Navajo soldiers. They would then translate their messages back into English.

The Japanese could never figure out the code.

In this way, Navajo soldiers helped win many battles.

♦♦♦

Prayer

Pray that more and more Navajos will understand the message of the Gospel and experience victory in Christ.

Day Two

The Navajos and Apaches came from Canada to the southwestern United States around the 1500s. At first, they raided Pueblo Indians for food and other goods. Although the Apaches continued to do this, the Navajos settled in permanent villages and raised animals instead.

Today, many Navajos still raise sheep. They still make baskets, pottery and jewelry. And many still live in cone-shaped houses called hogans.

The Navajos live on 29,000 square miles of reservation land, mostly in New Mexico, Arizona and Utah. The Navajo and Cherokee nations are the two largest tribes in the United States.

Navajos are also called Dineh (dee-NAY).

◆◆◆
Prayer
Pray that more and more Navajos will
follow Jesus as sheep follow their shepherd.

Manuelito

DAY THREE
In 1864, about 8,000 Navajos were rounded up by Kit Carson, legendary scout of the American West. The Navajos

were forced to leave northwestern New Mexico and northeastern Arizona.

It was the beginning of the "Long Walk" of the Navajos, a walk that took them over 300 miles from their homelands to eastern New Mexico. There, they were forced to live on a piece of land near the Pecos River.

The river water made the Navajos sick. They suffered from other diseases as well. Insects ate their corn. And there wasn't enough wood in the area to meet their needs.

Finally, after four years, the U.S. government let the Navajos go back to their original homelands.

♦♦♦
Prayer
Pray that the Navajos, other Indians, and all of us will forgive each other for the wicked things we have done and experience God's forgiveness in our own lives.

DAY FOUR

Indians today have a choice to make. First, they can choose to follow the traditional religions of their tribes. For the Navajos, this would mean worshiping many gods. It would mean being in bondage to evil spirits.

Second, they can choose to live for their own pleasures like many other Americans around them. Indians who follow this path usually add more problems to their lives, like alcoholism, broken families, and hurting children.

Third, they can choose to serve the Lord. A Navajo man named Raymond Perry has found hope in Christ. Now he preaches over television to other Indians in the southwest. This way the message of Jesus reaches even into Pueblo lands where such preaching is officially banned (see Week 28, Day Five, page 120)!

◆ ◆ ◆
Prayer

*Pray for Christian Navajos as they preach the gospel
and teach others what it means to follow Christ.*

DAY FIVE

In 1990, a group of Christian Indians traveled from America to Mongolia. It so happened that their tour guide was one of the few Christians in Mongolia at the time.

Some of the Indians visiting Mongolia were Navajos. They were invited by a Mongolian shepherd to share a meal with his family. The shepherd's family prepared the feast from start to finish, starting with a live goat.

When the Navajos saw how the Mongolians slaughtered their goats, they said that was just how they did it! When they saw how the Mongolians passed around the goat liver and fat, they said that was just how they did it!

At each point throughout the feast, the Navajos were amazed to see the Mongolians doing things the same way they would. They felt as if they had found long-lost brothers.

By the end of their time together, missionary Rick Leatherwood was asking the Mongolians if they wanted to receive forgiveness through Jesus, the Lamb of God. They all said they did!

◆ ◆ ◆
Prayer

*Pray that more and more Native American
Christians will go to other parts of the world
to tell people about new life in Jesus Christ.*

CALIFORNIA INDIANS

DAY ONE

If you fly into the Los Angeles airport for the first time, you may wonder what country you've landed in. There are so many different kinds of people living in California.

Even before people from around the globe came to California, there were many Indian tribes living there. The Yurok, Chumash, Miwoc, Pomo, Hupa, Yahi, Wintun and Yokuts are just some of the California Indian tribes.

The California Indians did not band together into one large tribe. They did not form confederacies like the Iroquois or councils like the Pueblos. Yet the small tribes got along well together and often traded with each other.

◆◆◆
Prayer
Thank God for giving His Only Son
for all the people groups of the world.

DAY TWO

Plenty of food was available to the California Indians, so they didn't need to grow many crops. They ate nuts, berries, seeds, greens, roots, and insects. They made flour from acorns, and boiled caterpillars in salt water. They hunted deer, rabbits, ducks, geese, and swans. They caught fish, and sometimes even hunted seals and sea otters.

The Indians enjoyed warm weather much of the time. But

when it was cold, they could put on robes made from sea otter furs, rabbit skins or feathers.

Some California Indians lived in small houses covered with bark. Others lived in dome-shaped pithouses covered with earth.

They got around by either walking or paddling their boats. The Yurok made dugout canoes carved from redwood logs. Others made rafts. The Chumash made boats from wooden planks.

◆ ◆ ◆
Prayer

Thank Jesus for being made in the likeness of men, walking dusty roads, traveling in boats and experiencing the kinds of things we experience.

DAY THREE

After the Spanish took over the Aztec Empire, they moved north to acquire more land. They entered the territory that is now Texas, New Mexico, Arizona, and California. It was 1542 when Spaniards first came to California.

The first Indians they met in California were the Chumash, who lived near the Santa Barbara channel. For the next two centuries, Spanish ships stopped in the Santa Barbara channel before crossing the Pacific Ocean to visit the Philippines, another area that Spain had claimed.

The Spanish, English and many other groups of people who eventually moved to California were all immigrants. They all come from somewhere else.

◆◆◆
Prayer
Pray that California Indians will know Jesus,
who left heaven to come to earth for them.

DAY FOUR

In the 1700s, Spanish missionaries built missions up and down the coast of California. The purpose of the missions was to convert Indians to Christianity and teach them how to grow crops.

The San Diego Mission was founded in 1769. Before long, a chain of twenty-one missions had been built from San Diego to San Francisco.

Spanish soldiers captured California Indians and forced them into slavery in the missions. They killed some of the Indians when they refused to cooperate with the soldiers. The Indians were taught to speak Spanish and were forced to build and farm for the Spaniards. The Indians who lived on the missions were called "mission Indians."

By 1834, the Spanish missionaries had abandoned the missions they had built. Unfortunately, many of the "mission Indians" had forgotten how their people used to live.

◆◆◆
Prayer
Pray that California Indians will know
Jesus, who took the form of a servant for them.

131

DAY FIVE

The Pomo tribe lived north of San Francisco, away from the missions. From 1811 to 1841, Russian fur traders operated a trading post in Pomo country. The Russians wanted Pomo men to hunt and clean hides for them, so they kidnapped Pomo women and children and held them hostage to frighten the men into doing work for them.

In 1848, California became part of the United States. In 1849, the gold rush began and white settlers streamed into California. These new immigrants took most of the Indians' land.

In 1850, two white men forced some Pomo Indians to work for them. The white men did not allow the Indians to hunt or fish. A number of Pomos died of starvation or beatings, and one Pomo was shot. After much discussion, some Pomo men decided to kill the two white men. In response, United States soldiers came and massacred two villages of Pomo people.

By 1850, two-thirds of the California Indians had died of disease, starvation, abuse or murder.

◆◆◆
Prayer
The California Indians have been so hurt by white Americans, they are unwilling to listen to much of anything they might have to say. Pray that God will provide messengers to whom the Indians can feel comfortable listening to the Good News about Jesus.

SHOSHONE

DAY ONE

Shoshone Indians were scattered over a wide area in the western United States. There are four main groups of Shoshones: Western, Northern, Eastern, and Comanche.

Western Shoshones lived in Nevada; Northern Shoshones in Idaho and Utah; Eastern Shoshones in Wyoming; and the Comanches broke off from the Eastern Shoshones and lived in Texas.

One day, some Hidatsa Indians (see Week 22, Day 2) raided the Eastern Shoshones. They kidnapped a young girl named Sacajawea (sack-uh-juh-WAY-uh) and eventually took her to the area that is now known as North Dakota. There she lived as a slave until a French-Canadian man bought her to be his wife.

◆◆◆
Prayer
Pray that the Shoshone will know the One
who came not to steal, but to give abundant life.

DAY TWO

The homeland of the Western Shoshones is called the Great Basin. It is a large area surrounded on all sides by mountains. The Paiute, Ute and Bannock tribes also lived in the Great Basin.

The Great Basin tribes all had similar lifestyles. They fished and gathered wild food. Because they dug in the ground for food, the Western Shoshones were called "Digger Indians."

The Eastern and Northern Shoshones lived like the Plains Indians and hunted buffalo.

In the early 1800s, there was an Eastern Shoshone chief named Cameahwait. Many members of his family had died. He had one brother and a nephew who were still living. He also had a sister who may have been alive. But she had been taken from her people when she was just a young girl.

◆◆◆

Prayer

Pray that the Shoshones will trust Jesus with their lives, knowing that He laid down His life for them.

DAY THREE

In 1803, after France sold to the United States the tract of land we know as the Louisiana Purchase, President Jefferson thought it would be a good idea to explore the land he had just purchased. Jefferson chose Captain Lewis and Captain Clark to lead the expedition. Lewis and Clark gathered supplies and recruited a team of men.

In May of 1804, the Lewis and Clark Expedition set out from St. Louis. They spent the winter in the Dakotas, where they were joined by Toussaint Charbonneau (TOO-san SHAR-buh-no) and his young wife.

In February of 1805, Mrs. Charbonneau gave birth to her first child, Jean Baptiste (ZHUN bap-TEEST). Two months later, father, mother and baby were on their way west with the Lewis and Clark Expedition.

Mrs. Charbonneau's first name was Sacajawea.

◆◆◆

Prayer

Pray that the Shoshones will let Jesus hold them and carry them through life.

DAY FOUR

One day as the Lewis and Clark expedition was traveling by river, a storm tipped one of the boats on its side. Packages of important instruments fell into the water. Sacajawea, with Jean Baptiste on her back, scooped up the packages while the men pushed the boat back down.

According to diaries of the men on the trip, Sacajawea realized they were in an area near her childhood home. She directed the explorers to her tribe, the Eastern Shoshone. Lewis and Clark were hoping the Shoshones would sell them some horses so they could get across the mountains.

What a surprise for Chief Cameahwait! His sister had come with a bunch of explorers! Of course he would sell horses to them. He drew a map, and even sent a helper, Old Toby, along with them. With the horses, the map and the help of Old Toby, the expedition made it through the mountains.

The Lewis and Clark Expedition eventually reached the Pacific Ocean and then returned to St. Louis. Without Sacajawea's help, however, they might not have made it!

♦♦♦

Prayer
Pray that the Shoshones will
follow Jesus, listening to His voice.

DAY FIVE

During the 1860s, Indians of the Great Basin fought to stop the stream of white people who were heading west through their territory. Western Shoshones and other Indians attacked miners, settlers, wagon trains and stagecoaches.

The Eastern Shoshones, on the other hand, kept peace with the whites. Their leader, Chief Washakie, figured that keeping peace was the best road to survival for his people.

In 1868, the Eastern Shoshones were given the Wind River reservation in Wyoming. It was the only time in U.S. history that Indians were permitted to choose the location of their reservation.

Today, about 10,000 Shoshones live on reservations in Nevada, California, Utah, Idaho and Wyoming.

◆◆◆

Prayer

*Pray that many Shoshones will choose Jesus
and receive the eternal life He offers.*

NEZ PERCE

DAY ONE

The Nez Perce (nez PERS) were peaceful Indians who were open to new ideas.

They lived mainly in Idaho and Oregon, in an area called the Plateau. The Spokane, Thompson, Walla Walla, Palouse, Yakima, Salish and Cayuse tribes also lived on the Plateau.

When horses came to the Plateau area, the Indians figured out how to use them. They became excellent horsemen.

The Cayuses raised spotted Appaloosas. The Nez Perces, at one time, owned the largest herd of horses on the continent.

♦♦♦

Prayer
*Pray that the hearts of the Nez Perce
Indians will be open to the love of Jesus.*

DAY TWO

During the winter, the Nez Perces lived in earth-covered pithouses. A few families lived in each house, and five or six houses would make up a village.

During the summer, they lived in portable houses covered with woven plant material. Summer was the time when they went hunting.

The Nez Perces liked to hunt buffalo on the plains, but the Crow Indians had driven them into the mountains, so they began to hunt elk, deer, mountain sheep and rabbits.

In 1805, the Shoshone Indian, Old Toby, guided the Lewis and Clark Expedition to where the Nez Perce tribe lived. The Nez Perce Indians were very helpful to Lewis and Clark.

◆ ◆ ◆
Prayer
Pray that the Nez Perce Indians will welcome those who come to show them God's love.

DAY THREE

The Nez Perce Indians wanted to live at peace with whites. In order to keep peace, they gave up portions of their land. In exchange, the white immigrants promised them schools, money, livestock and tools. The U.S. government also promised that the Nez Perce could keep the rest of their land.

In 1831, newspapers reported that four Nez Perce Indians had come to St. Louis looking for the "Whiteman's Book of Heaven." The article called for missionaries to go to the Nez Perce. Several people responded.

Some of the missionaries lived among the Nez Perce and became friends with Chief Old Joseph. The Nez Perce were friendly and eager to learn from the missionaries. Many, including Old Joseph, accepted the Christian message.

◆ ◆ ◆
Prayer
Pray that the hearts of the Nez Perce Indians will once again be hungry for the truth of God's Word.

DAY FOUR

In 1860, miners began taking more land from the Nez Perce. They wanted the gold they had found there. In 1863, the Nez Perce gave up more land to keep peace. Up to this point,

Chief Joseph

they had never killed a white person. But when Old Joseph learned that the whites were trying to take even more of his homeland, he tore up his Bible and renounced Christianity.

After Old Joseph died in 1871, his son became Chief Joseph.

Things got worse. The only land the Nez Perce had left was the Wallowa Valley. Prospectors moved in there, too.

For the first time in their history, the Nez Perce killed some whites...and U.S. troops responded by attacking the Nez Perce. The Nez Perce fled into the wilderness.

♦ ♦ ♦
Prayer
Pray that the hearts of the Nez Perce
Indians will find refuge in Christ.

DAY FIVE

U.S. troops chased the Nez Perce for 1,700 miles through Idaho, Wyoming and Montana. The Nez Perce tried to escape to Canada. Many died along the way, and the rest were tired and hungry. U.S. Army troops caught up with the Nez Perce just 30 miles away from Canada.

After six days of fighting, Chief Joseph surrendered. He said, "I am tired of fighting. Our chiefs are killed. It is cold and we have no blankets. The little children are freezing. I am tired. I will fight no more forever." Only 418 of the 4,000 Nez Perce were still alive.

The Nez Perce were sent to Kansas and then to Oklahoma. Disease took more lives. In 1885, the 257 surviving Nez Perce Indians were allowed to go to a reservation in Washington State.

In 1904, Chief Joseph died. The reservation doctor said he died of a broken heart.

Before his death, Chief Joseph rejected Christianity and returned to his traditional religion.

♦ ♦ ♦
Prayer
Pray that the hearts of the Nez Perce
Indians will forgive and be healed.

NORTHWEST COASTAL INDIANS

DAY ONE

Many tribes lived along the coast where Oregon, Washington, British Columbia and Alaska are today. Among them: the Tlingit, Nootka, Makah, Chinook, Salish, Cowichan, Nanaimo, Bella Coola, Tsimshian and Haida peoples.

These tribes found a wealth of food and supplies along the Pacific Coast. They caught herrings, tunas, cods, seals, otters, sea lions and dolphins in the ocean. They harvested clams and bird eggs along the shorelines.

They fished for salmon in the nearby rivers. And they hunted deer, mountain goat, elk, bear, beaver, muskrat and squirrel in the forests.

◆◆◆
Prayer
Pray that Coastal Indians will put their hope in
God, who richly supplies us with all things to enjoy.

DAY TWO

Not only was there a wealth of food in the ocean, but the land along the coast also held a wealth of supplies for the Indians.

Great trees grew in the forests. The Indians used logs to build homes.

Animals provided furs. The Indians were able to trade furs

141

with French, Russian, Spanish and English traders. In exchange, they received iron products, like knives.

The Indians thought certain animals protected them. They carved images of these animals in logs, making the logs into totem poles.

◆◆◆
Prayer
Pray that Coastal Indians will be saved
through faith in Christ, because of the riches
of God's grace and the greatness of His love.

DAY THREE

Wealth was important to the Coastal Indians. A person's wealth was seen as proof of his hard work, skill or fighting ability. But it was not enough merely to have wealth. The

Indians considered it a great honor to be able to give. And wealthy people had more to give away.

For special occasions, such as a marriage, birth or burial, an Indian family would host a big ceremony called a potlatch. A potlatch might last for days, and there could be hundreds of guests. The purpose of the potlatch was to give wealth away to others.

The more a host gave away, the greater he was in the eyes of his guests. He would give gifts of canoes, sealskins, whale oil, or slaves. At the end of the ceremony, the guests would give gifts to the host.

This type of giving helped to provide for families who were not as wealthy.

◆ ◆ ◆

Prayer
Pray that Coastal Indians will
know Jesus Christ who, though He was rich,
became poor so that we might become rich.

DAY FOUR

The Tlingit Indians lived where Alaska is today. They were traders and whalers. Tlingit, Nootka and Makah Indians all hunted for whales. One whale could supply enough food and oil for a whole village.

The Tlingits were also warriors. If others did something against the Tlingits, they considered war as a way to "get even." They also went to war to take things from others.

Like many peoples, the Tlingits had special ceremonies to mark the time when a child became an adult. Ceremonies like these are called rites of passage. Even though they are celebrating the same thing, rites of passage are often different for different tribes.

Sometimes rites of passage are connected with a tribe's religious beliefs. When Indians become Christians, this is one area they often find they need to pray about. They need to ask God for wisdom to know how to honor Him in their celebrations of life's changes.

◆◆◆
Prayer

Pray that Coastal Indians who are Christians will ask for wisdom from God, who gives to all men generously.

DAY FIVE

In 1741, the Russian explorer Bering claimed Alaska for Russia. In 1799, the Russians built a fort at Sitka.

The Tlingits viewed the Russians as invaders and thieves. In 1802, the Tlingits captured the Russian fort at Sitka. They killed many Russians and took thousands of fur pelts. The Tlingits thought of the furs as their own, because they came from animals on Tlingit lands.

Later, the Russians took the fort back, but the Tlingits kept fighting against them. The resistance of the Tlingits was one reason why the Russians sold Alaska to the United States in 1867.

◆◆◆
Prayer

Pray that Coastal Indians who are Christians will know the true riches of the glory of God's inheritance in them.

CHIPEWYAN

DAY ONE

The Chipewyan (chip-uh-WY-an) Indians lived in the taiga (TY-geh) area of Canada. The taiga reaches from the Rocky Mountains to the Atlantic Ocean. It is covered with forests, lakes, rivers, swamps and ponds.

The Chipewyan, Yellowknife, Dogrib, Beaver and other tribes lived in the northwestern part of the taiga.

The taiga is just one part of the North American Subarctic, the region just south of the Arctic. The mountains of Alaska, the Yukon Territory, and British Columbia make up another part. The third part is the tundra—the flatter land near the coasts. The tundra is frozen most of the year.

♦♦♦
Prayer
*Pray that the Chipewyan Indians will not see this world
as their home, but that they will be prepared
to go to heaven someday to be with Jesus.*

DAY TWO

In a land of long winters and short summers, farming was not possible. So hunting was a way of life for tribes living in the taiga. Chipewyans and other Indians depended on animals for their food and clothing.

Beavers, muskrats, foxes, deer, wolves, bears, moose and caribou are just some of the animals that live in this northern region.

Caribous look like big deer. Just as buffaloes were important to the Plains Indians, caribous were important to the Chipewyan and other tribes of the north.

◆◆◆
Prayer
Pray that the Chipewyan Indians will be concerned not only about food and clothing, but that they will seek first the kingdom of God.

DAY THREE

Caribou provided the Chipewyans with meat for food, bones for tools, skins for clothing and shelter, and tendons for bow strings.

Indians like the Chipewyans followed the caribou north during the warm seasons and south during the cold seasons. They lived in portable tents similar to tepees.

The Chipewyans had lots of tricks for hunting caribou. Sometimes they would drive them into corrals. Sometimes they would catch them with ropes strung between trees. Other times they would find the caribou swimming in lakes and rivers and shoot them from their canoes.

They even learned to bang antlers together, which tricked caribou bulls into thinking that other bulls were fighting over a female. The bulls would come running... right into a trap.

◆◆◆
Prayer
Pray that the Chipewyans will not think only of time and seasons, but of eternity.

DAY FOUR

Chipewyan men did the hunting and fishing, built canoes and made tools. The women tended fires, did the cooking, cut up the hunted animals, dried the meat, tanned the skins, and made clothing.

If it weren't for animals, the Chipewyans would have had a hard time finding food or making clothes. If it weren't for the men, the women and children would have had a hard time catching the animals.

So the women treated their men specially. If there was not enough food, the women didn't eat.

Whenever possible, the Chipewyans would feed their dogs

147

well. Dogs were given special honor. This is because the Chipewyans believed that human beings originally came from dogs.

◆ ◆ ◆

Prayer

Pray that the Chipewyans will know they did not come from dogs, but that they have been created in the image of God, to praise and glorify Him.

DAY FIVE

Chipewyans were helpful to European fur traders. Chipewyan guides helped the traders find their way.

However, the French traders sold guns to the Crees before selling them to the Chipewyans. The Crees were the enemies of the Chipewyans. With guns, the Crees were able to drive the Chipewyans further to the northwest.

Fur traders also brought diseases. In 1781, smallpox killed more than half of the Chipewyan people.

Today, the Chipewyans have reservations in Alberta, Saskatchewan, Manitoba, and the Northwest Territories of Canada. Many Chipewyans still hunt as a way of life.

◆ ◆ ◆

Prayer

Pray that the Chipewyan will not look to anything in this world for security, but that they will look to Jesus.

HAWAIIANS

The Hawaiians are usually left out of any discussion of American Indians. This is probably because Hawaii is not part of the continental Americas. They are included here, however, because they were native to their land before white people arrived and because today their land is part of the United States. Their history is part of the history of the United States.

DAY ONE

Shortly after the time of Christ, brave explorers from Polynesia set out in boats on the Pacific Ocean. They came to a cluster of eight small islands and decided to settle there. The islands were actually the tops of underwater mountains formed by volcanoes.

Around 1000 AD, some people from Tahiti also came to the islands. They became the rulers and priests.

In Polynesian culture, relationships are very important. Harmony between people is an important part of their spiritual beliefs.

Today, the descendants of these early island dwellers are known as Hawaiians.

♦♦♦
Prayer
Pray that Hawaiians will be one in Christ by putting their faith in Him.

DAY TWO

With plenty of rain, sunshine and good soil, the Hawaiian Islands produce a bountiful supply of food. Early islanders enjoyed coconuts, breadfruits, sugar cane, sweet potatoes and bananas.

With food so plentiful, the Hawaiians didn't have to spend much time growing it or looking for it. They had plenty of time to develop their relationships with each other and to develop their skills in making beautiful things.

The Hawaiians used their talents to help each other. They thought of each member of the community as part of a big family, or *ohana*. The word *aloha* refers to the love and compassion shared by everyone in the big ohana.

◆◆◆
Prayer
Pray that many Hawaiians will become members of God's ohana *through Christ.*

DAY THREE

In 1555, the Spanish navigator Gaetano put the Hawaiian Islands on a map.

In 1778, the British Captain Cook visited the islands. When he landed at Kealakekua Bay, the Hawaiians were having a great festival to honor a god. They thought Captain

Cook was that god. Cook went along with it and received many gifts from the Hawaiians.

La ter, a storm damaged his ships. Captain Cook had to go back to the same bay for repairs. Broken down ships did not impress the Hawaiians. They stole a small boat, and Cook tried to get it back. This time, instead of being honored, he was killed.

◆◆◆
Prayer
Pray that Hawaiians will know the only true
God, and Jesus Christ whom He has sent.

DAY FOUR

The first Christian missionaries arrived in Hawaii in 1820. Sadly, they did not always set a good example. Missionaries and other whites built plantations and factories for themselves. It wasn't long before the islands were owned and run mainly by whites.

But some Hawaiians did believe the gospel. Queen Kapiolani put her faith in the true God and did not fear anyone but Him.

One of the gods of the Hawaiians was called Pele. Hawaiians believed that the eruption of the volcano Kilauea was a demonstration of the anger of Pele.

Queen Kapiolani stood at the top of this volcano and told her people that Jehovah was her God. She told them that she did not fear Pele, but trusted in Jehovah. Jehovah God protected her.

◆◆◆
Prayer
Thank God for Hawaiians who do know the true
God. Pray for others who will believe in Christ
because of the testimony of those who know Him.

DAY FIVE

The Hawaiian Islands were united under one ruler, Kamehameha, in 1810.

In 1893, a group of white businessmen, with the help of U.S. Marines, overthrew Hawaii's Queen Liliuokalani. The businessmen declared themselves the leaders of Hawaii.

President Cleveland called the takeover a disgrace, and said Queen Liliuokalani should be returned to power. She never was.

The next president, William McKinley, supported the white American government in Hawaii.

In 1900, Hawaii was established as a U.S. territory. In 1959, it became the fiftieth state.

In 1993, the U.S. Congress officially apologized to the Hawaiian people for taking over their country.

◆◆◆

Prayer

Pray that the United States will do what is right concerning Hawaii. Pray that, as Christians, we will submit to the authority of Jesus Christ, letting Him live in us, that the love of God will truly be seen in our actions.

PICTURE CREDITS

Illustrations found on the pages listed below were derived from the sources cited.

10 Mayan mother and child: *Insight Guide: Guatemala, Belize & The Yucatan* (Singapore: Apa Publications GmbH & Co., 2000) 73. **35** Four Beauties of Cape Prince of Wales: Culver Pictures, Inc. **38** Oklahoma Hunter: W.S. Prettyman, Oklahoma Historical Society/Archives Division, No. 20768. **51** Choctaw singers: *Insight Guides, Native America* (Hong Kong: Apa Publications GmbH & Co., 1991) 306, 307. **54** Ojibwa man: National Archives, 1898. **58** Cree Indian in front of tepee: Notman Photo, Provincial Archives of Manitoba. **67** Oneida woman weaving a basket: Smithsonian Institution/National Anthropological Archives. **74** Potawatomi: W.S. Prettyman, Western History Collections, University of Oklahoma, Prettyman 156. **83** Cherokee girl: Smithsonian Institution. **90** Osage girl, Smithsonian Institution. **106** Cheyenne warrior near rocks: Smithsonian Institution. **114** Paiute seed gatherer: John Hillers, National Archives, 1873. **119** Edward S. Curtis, "Jicarilla Girl," Library of Congress, Washington, DC, 1905. **123** Geronimo: Smithsonian Institution National Anthropological Archives. **135** Shoshone woman: Baker and Johnston, Wyoming State Archives. **142** Tlingit from Yakutat: American Museum of Natural History, 1904. **147** Chipewyan family with their dogs: J.B. Tyrell, Provincial Archives of Manitoba, 1894.

ADDITIONAL RESOURCES

POWHATAN
www.patc.net/history/native/ind_hist.html

INUIT
Transformations II, George Otis, Jr.

DELAWARE
www.delawaretribeofindians.nsn.us/faq.html
www.burlco.lib.nj.us/county/history/native.html
*A History of the Expansion of Christianity, Vol. 3: "Three Centuries
of Advance: 1500 A.D. to 1800 A.D.*, by Kenneth Scott Latourette,
Zondervan Publishing House, Grand Rapids, Michigan, copyright
1967 by Harper & Row, Publishers; Zondervan CEP Edition; seventh
edition printed 1980, pp. 221-222.
www.wholesomewords.org/missions/biobrainerd2.html

LUMBEE
[1] www.indyweek.com/durham/2000-12-06/cover.html
[2] www.nativealliance.org/mt_haven.html
[3] http://denix.cecer.army.mil/denix/Public/Native/Outreach/
American/indian.html
[4] www.lumbee.org/recognition.htm
[5] www.lumbee.org/faq.htm

CHOCTAW
[1] www.choctawnation.com/history/trail_of_tears.htm
[2] *Whiteman's Gospel*, by Craig Stephen Smith, Indian Life Books,
Winnipeg, Manitoba, Canada, © 1997, p. 51.

CHIPPEWA

1 www.boisforte.com/partnerships/regulations.html
2 www.perm.org/articles/a068.html
3 www.ecm-inc.com/news/postreview/2000/august/23Rice.html
4 www.musicoutfitters.com/bwcaw.htm
5 www.kstrom.net/isk/maps/mn/treaties.html
6 For more information, see *Boundary Lines*, "The Official Guidelines of the Official Workers and Member Congregations of the Native American District of the Christian and Missionary Alliance (US)." *Boundary Lines* deals with "The Issue of Christ, Indigenous Worship, and Native American Culture." Craig Smith is the superintendent of the Native American District of the Christian and Missionary Alliance. See web site: www.nativealliance.org/products.html.

CREE

1 www.illuminart.com/wycliffe/news/index.asp?DocumentID=45

IROQUOIS

1 www.geocities.com/Athens/Olympus/3808/about.html
2 *Whiteman's Gospel*, by Craig Smith, Life Books, Winnipeg, Manitoba, Canada, © 1997, p. 42.
3 www.lucy.ukc.ac.uk/EthnoAtlas/Hmar/Cult_dir/Culture.7849

HURON & OTTAWA

1 http://wire.dailynews.net/ottawa/2000/baptist.html

POTAWATOMI

1 www.geocities.com/the_wanderling/midewiwin.html

MIAMI & SHAWNEE

1 www.ifa-usapray.org/Features/Zero%20Year%20Curse%20Broken.html

CHEROKEE
[1] *Whiteman's Gospel*, by Craig Smith, Indian Life Books, Winnipeg, Manitoba, Canada, © 1997, p. 46.

CHICKASAW
[1] "First Encounter - de Soto Meets the Chickasaws," by Tom Phillips, © 1995. See www.chickasaw.net/culture/art/firsten.htm.

CROW
[1] *Whiteman's Gospel*, by Craig Stephen Smith, Indian Life Books, Winnipeg, Manitoba, Canada, 1997, p. 143.

BLACKFEET
[1] www.umt.edu/globalfirenet/chiefmtn.html
[2] www.blackfeetnation.com/Home%20Page/timeline.htm
[3] www.frontiernet.net/~brez13/buffalo.htm
[4] www.thefirstamericans.homestead.com/Buffalo.html

PAWNEE
[1] www.trailsoftears.org/tribalinfo/content-pawnee.htm
[2] www.pawneenation.org/history.html

PAIUTE & UTE
[1] ww.dreamscape.com/morgana/wknee.htm

PUEBLO
[1] www.aipcinc.com/history/htm
[2] www.cmalliance.org/missions/world/upgs/pgfiles/029.htm
[3] http://home.earthlink.net/~acolville/

APACHE
[1] *Whiteman's Gospel*, by Craig Stephen Smith, Indian Life Books, Winnipeg, Manitoba, Canada, 1997, p. 142.

NAVAJO

[1] *Smithsonian Magazine*, 1997. All rights reserved. www.smith
sonianmag.si.edu/smithsonian/issues97/dec97/bosque.html
[2] *Whiteman's Gospel*, by Craig Stephen Smith, Indian Life Books,
Winnipeg, Manitoba, Canada, 1997, p. 133ff.
[3] www.missionfrontiers.org/1990/12/d907.htm

CALIFORNIA INDIANS

[1] www.geocities.com/bloodyisland2000/indianview.htm

SHOSHONE

[1] www.carmensandiego.com/products/time/lewisclarkc15/
shoshoni.html
[2] www.rootsweb.com/~nwa/sacajawea.html
[3] www.wind-river.org/windriverreservation.htm

NEZ PERCE

[1] www.rootsweb.com/~nwa/sacajawea.html

HAWAIIANS

[1] www.fair-wind.com/history.html
[2] www.vrmaui.com/pray4hawaii/kapi.html
[3] www.geocities.com/kanekula/hawaii/timeline.html
[4] www.hawaii-nation.org/betrayal.html